Florian Förg

Seeing the Unseen

Dortmunder Beiträge zu Theologie und Religionspädagogik

herausgegeben von

Prof. Dr. Michael Basse

und

Prof. Dr. Thomas Pola

Band 16

LIT

Florian Förg

Seeing the Unseen

Ezekiel's Visions in a Thai Context

LIT

Cover image: *Ezekiel* by Sawai Chinnawong;
photo taken by Wachana Puchai

This book is printed on acid-free paper.

Bibliographic information published by the Deutsche Nationalbibliothek
The Deutsche Nationalbibliothek lists this publication in the Deutsche Nationalbibliografie; detailed bibliographic data are available in the Internet at http://dnb.dnb.de.

ISBN 978-3-643-91251-0 (pb)
ISBN 978-3-643-96251-5 (PDF)

A catalogue record for this book is available from the British Library.

Klosbachstr. 107
CH-8032 Zürich
Tel. +41 (0) 44-251 75 05
E-Mail: zuerich@lit-verlag.ch http://www.lit-verlag.ch

Distribution:

In the UK: Global Book Marketing, e-mail: mo@centralbooks.com
In North America: Independent Publishers Group, e-mail: orders@ipgbook.com
In Germany: LIT Verlag Fresnostr. 2, D-48159 Münster
Tel. +49 (0) 2 51-620 32 22, Fax +49 (0) 2 51-922 60 99, e-mail: vertrieb@lit-verlag.de

e-books are available at www.litwebshop.de

To Judith

Contents

Abbreviations

AncB	Anchor Bible
ESV	English Standard Version
FOTL	Forms of Old Testament Literature
ICC	International Critical Commentary
KJV	King James Version
LXX	Septuagint
NICOT	New International Commentary on the Old Testament
NIV	New International Version
MT	Masoretic Text
THSV 1977	Thai Standard Version (1977)
THSV 2011	Thai Standard Version (2011)
TNCV	Thai New Contemporary Version
TDOT	Theological Dictionary of the Old Testament
WBC	Word Biblical Commentary

The transcription of Thai words follows the standard of the Royal Thai General System of Transcription in the version of 1999 which has been published by the Royal Institute of Thailand.[1] The tran-

---

1 https://en.wikipedia.org/wiki/Royal_Thai_General_System_of_Transcription#cite_ref-6.

scription of Hebrew terms follows the academic style pattern as described in the SBL Handbook of Style.[2]

If not stated otherwise, all citations from the Bible are taken from the Thai Standard Version of 2011 and from the English Standard Version.

---

[2] Billie Jean Collins and Society of Biblical Literature, *The SBL Handbook of Style*, 2nd ed. (Atlanta: SBL Press, 2014), 26-28.

Preface

This book first came into being as a result of a research project funded by Payap University in Chiang Mai, Thailand. For printing some changes have been made. The original title of the project was "The Use of the Thai Term *nimit* for the Hebrew Terms *ḥāzôn*, *mar'ê,* and *maḥăzê* in the Book of Ezekiel". This was made possible by the cooperation of many people who gave their encouragement, information, suggestions, advice, and opinions.

I would first like to thank the specialists who were involved in the research process from the beginning: Rev. Dr. Satanun Boonyakiat, Dr. Chaiyun Ukosakul, and Dr. Brian Lima. They kindly read the research draft and helped me to get a clear focus on the topic and the scope of research. Besides that, they also read and gave valuable comments on the research paper. Without their passionate participation and input, the research project could not have been successfully conducted. I also thank Rev. Dr. Ernst Horn who kindly read the paper as an external examiner and enriched the discussion in the final defense meeting.

I am grateful to Dr. Sakunee Kriangchaiporn who helped in writing the research draft and coordinated the communication between McGilvary College of Divinity and the Research Office at Payap University. Besides that, the door to her office was always open whenever I had a question about my research or writing. Her advice has been inspiring to me and encouraged me a lot.

I would like to express my thankfulness to Khun Kobgarn Phochaachai at the Research Office of Payap University who has been a great and generous help in coordinating every step of the whole research process.

Furthermore, I would like to give thanks to Rangsima Khamsan, the librarian of the Dewald Memorial Library (McGilvary-College of Divinity). Her unfailing support in searching for books has saved me many working hours.

My special thanks and appreciation go to William Hanna and Keegan West, who proofread the research report and gave insightful comments.

Prof. Dr. Thomas Pola and Prof. Dr. Michael Basse (Dortmund University) kindly allowed this book to be published in “Dortmunder Beiträge zu Theologie und Religionspädagogik”. I therefore would like to thank them cordially.

The picture on the cover has been painted by Saway Chinnawong. I am very thankful for his successful contribution that builds a bridge between Ezekiel as a prophet and Thai culture. The photo for the book cover was taken from this artwork by Wachana Puchai.

Finally, I express my profound gratitude to my family; first of all to my wife Katrin, who encouraged me not to give up when the next step in the research process was unclear or the work with Ezekiel took longer than expected. My daughter Judith (Nong Mina) also helped me with her laughter to forget about the difficulties of this project. Thanks to both of you!

Florian Förg

December 2019

1 Introduction

1.1 Background and Objectives

Some prophets in the Old Testament claim to have received visions. This is especially true of Daniel and Ezekiel, whose books have large sections that include visions (Dn 2-7, about half of the Book of Daniel and Ezekiel 1-3:15; 8-11; 37:1-11; 40-48, roughly one third of the book). Besides Daniel and Ezekiel, Amos and Zechariah also recorded the visions they received from God (Am 7-9; Zec 1:7-6:8, also known as the "Eight Night Visions")

In my Old Testament teaching at Payap University (CT 521/522 Old Testament 1 and 2; CT 322/725 Selected Old Testament Books) the English textbooks usually call these texts "visions", whereas some Thai textbooks use the word นิมิต (*nimit*). Some textbooks use *nimit* in two ways: Firstly for visions in the true sense of the word, where the prophet is recording what he has seen: e.g. the heavenly realm, angels, the glory of Yahweh, or future events that are given in symbols. This fits well to the original meaning of the word "vision" that is derived from Latin "videre" which means "to see".

Secondly, the word *nimit* is used for reports of information that the prophet has heard audibly from God (auditions), the result being that *nimit* is used more often: In total Ezekiel received 13 visions, i.e. *nimit*.[1]

Having these two uses of *nimit* in mind, one might get the impression that *nimit* is used for both visions (godly information that the

---

[1] Immanuel Scharrer, *An Introduction to the 16 Prophetical Books* (Chiang Mai: Faculty of Theology, Payap University, 1997), 164 [in Thai].

prophet receives through seeing) and auditions (received to the prophet by hearing).

In addition, the word *nimit* is used in Thailand to describe the future plans of a church. "The vision of our church is to plant five new churches in the next ten years". I suspect that these future action plans of churches do not fit with the meaning of *nimit* in the Old Testament. Besides *nimit,* some churches also use the word วิสัยทัศน์ (*wisaithat*) to express their plans for the future.

The observations above lead to the impression that there is a confusion of terms concerning vision reports in the Old Testament. More than that, this confusion of terms turns out to be a hindrance in understanding vision reports in the Bible. Besides that, the meaning and the concepts behind the Thai word *nimit* and the Hebrew words used for vision might differ and thus lead to even more confusion.

Against this background the present study attempts to achieve the following objectives: 1. To clarify the meanings of the terms חָזוֹן (*ḥāzôn*), מַרְאֶה (*mar'ê*) and מַחֲזֶה (*maḥăzê*) in the Book of Ezekiel. 2. To study the use of the Thai word *nimit* in translating *ḥāzôn, mar'ê,* and *maḥăzê*. 3. To investigate what happened when Ezekiel received a vision(s). 4. To give suggestions on how to communicate the concepts behind *ḥāzôn, mar'ê,* and *maḥăzê* effectively to Thai Christians. In order to achieve the objectives set out above, the present study will proceed as follows:

1.2 Methodology and Scope

First of all, this study will investigate in which verses the Book of Ezekiel uses the words *ḥāzôn*, *mar'ê,* and *maḥăzê*.

Even though the basic meaning of the roots of the Hebrew terms (ראה *r-'-h* and חזה *ḥ-z-h*) will be clarified in chapter 2.6 and 2.7 (see p. 24ff. and 26f.), the present study will then in a second step investigate the meaning of *ḥāzôn*, *mar'ê,* and *maḥăzê*. This is important as it is possible that a specific meaning of one of the words is only a minor aspect of the root.

The next step will be to take all the occurrences of *ḥāzôn*, *mar'ê,* and *maḥăzê* as found in the Book of Ezekiel and study which word(s) are used in the Thai translation. The Thai Standard Version of 2011 will serve as a basis in this step for two primary reasons. The first, is that it is one of the most recent Thai Bible translations (a revision of an earlier edition in 1971). The second, is that The Church of Christ in Thailand (CCT), the largest Protestant denomination in Thailand, recommends this version to be used in the services of its member churches.

Additionally, there might be more occurrences of *nimit* in the Thai translation that *do not* have *ḥāzôn*, *mar'ê,* and *maḥăzê* in the Hebrew. Therefore, it is necessary to search for all the occurrences of *nimit* in the Thai translation and check which words the Hebrew text is using. If it should turn out that there are more words than *ḥāzôn*, *mar'ê,* and *maḥăzê* that are translated as *nimit* in the Thai translation, the study should be extended in order to include those words as well.

In order to clarify what happened when Ezekiel received a vision, the current study will examine the introductory and closing sections of the vision reports in the book of Ezekiel, as those texts contain detailed information concerning the process of receiving a vision. In doing exegesis, the present study will deal with the final text as we have it in the Hebrew Bible and will not go into literary criticism, source criticism, or redaction criticism. Instead, the focus will be on the meaning of words and the analysis of the context, the historical background, and the connections of the texts to other parts of the Book of Ezekiel.

The main body of the visionary texts in the Book of Ezekiel contains additional information about the concepts behind visions and the receiving of them. Therefore, this study will exegete the visionary texts in the Book of Ezekiel. However, as the visions have many chapters, the exegesis cannot go deep in the present paper. I will instead deal with the sections that are most important for the present paper and focus on the theological message of the visionary texts as a whole.

As a final step, possibilities and ideas for how the findings can be taught to the Christians in Thailand will be developed. It is my estimate that the outcome will not be a fixed strategy, but more likely a collection of ideas that will help the Christians in Thailand to better understand the visions of the Book of Ezekiel. Also included in this section will be a short study of the meaning of the Thai word *nimit*, as the meaning of the Thai word will always be the first thing Thai Christians think about when talking about visions in the Old Testament.

The present study is an attempt to clarify these issues by focusing on the Book of Ezekiel. This biblical book has been chosen because visions play an important role in the Book of Ezekiel: 16 chapters and 11 verses out of a total of 48 chapters are visionary reports. Scholars agree that Ezekiel recorded four visions that he received from God: Ez 1–3; 8–11; 37:1–11 and ch. 40–48. When it seems appropriate, texts from other books of the Bible will be consulted as well. However, this study will not include pseudepigraphal writings such as the Book of Enoch with its long visionary reports, nor the cultural surroundings of Israel like ancient Egypt, Mesopotamia or Greece.

2 Ezekiel, His Visions and His Book

2.1 Ezekiel the Prophet

The most important text we have about Ezekiel as a person is Ez 1:1–3, which is, simultaneously, the introduction to the first report of Ezekiel's visionary experiences in Ez 1:1–3:15. Additionally, in Ezekiel 2:1-3:11, we find his calling.

> *Ez 1:1* In the thirtieth year, in the fourth month, on the fifth day of the month, as I was among the exiles by the Chebar canal, the heavens were opened, and I saw visions of God.
> 2 On the fifth day of the month (it was the fifth year of the
> exile of King Jehoiachin), 3 the word of the Lord came to Ezekiel the priest, the son of Buzi, in the land of the Chaldeans by the Chebar canal, and the hand of the Lord was upon him there.

According to Ez 1:3, the word of God came to "*Ezekiel the priest, the son of Buzi*". The Hebrew however has another word order ("*Ezekiel, the son of Buzi, the priest*") and is thus not clear whether Ezekiel himself was a priest, or his father Buzi was. At the very least, Ezekiel came from a priestly family. However, we have to consider the fact that in ancient societies like Israel, the son usually learnt the profession of his father. So, if Ezekiel's father Buzi was a priest, then it seems likely that Ezekiel himself was a priest as well.[1] The main reason for this is his profound knowledge about Yahweh's temple in Jerusalem, which is reflected in his visionary reports in Ez 8–11 and 40–48.

V. 1 mentions that Ezekiel is among the exiled Jews in Babylon. There were at least two times in Israelite history when the Babylonians deported Jews to the Babylonian mainland.

---

[1] Tremper III Longman and Raymond B. Dillard, *An Introduction to the Old Testament* (Grand Rapids: Zondervan, 2006), 354.

The first time was in 597 B.C. (2 Kgs 24:14-17), when King Nebuchadnezzar of Babylonia exiled King Jehoiachin, members of the upper class, soldiers, craftsmen and smiths.

In the second deportation of 586 B.C., Nebuzaradan, one of the high officials of Nebuchadnezzar, destroyed Jerusalem including the temple and the city walls after two years of besieging the city (2 Kgs 25:8-10). In addition, he exiled King Zedekiah (v. 4-7) and all the population of Jerusalem except for the poor in Jerusalem who worked as vinedressers and plowmen (2 Kgs 25:11-12). Besides that, upper class citizens of Jerusalem were brought to Riblah at the border of Israel and were killed there by the King of Babylon (2 Kgs 25:18-21).

According to Jer 52:30, Nebuzaradan sent Judeans into exile in 582 B.C. for the third time.

"A fourth deportation dating to the reign of Jehojakim, antedating the three noted above, is reported in 2 Chr 36:6-7 and Dn 1:1-17, but seems unlikely to modern historians".[2] This would have been in the third year of King Jehojakim (Dn 1:1; 605 B.C.).

Along with King Jehoiachin, the prophet Ezekiel was brought to Babylonia in the first deportation of 597 B.C. (Ez 1:2) and stayed in the colony of exiled Jews at the Chebar canal (v. 1). In the fifth year of his (and King Jehoiachin's) exile, in 593 B.C., he started to see visions of God and in the first vision God called Ezekiel to be a prophet (Ez 2:1–3:11). The "thirtieth year" (Ez 1:1) probably relates to the age of the prophet in that year, so that Ezekiel would have been born in 623 B.C.

Ezekiel's ministry in Babylonia continued at least until 571 B.C. This fact can be seen from the fact that the youngest of all the very exactly dated oracles in the Book of Ezekiel dates from the "twen-

---

[2] Ralph W. Klein, "Exile," in *The New Interpreters® Dictionary of the Bible* 2, ed. Katharine Doob Sakenfield et al. (Nashville: Abingdon Press, 2009), 367.

ty-seventh year, in the first month, on the first day of the month" (Ez 29:17). As the counting of the years starts anew in the year of Ezekiel's calling, the 27th year is 571 B.C.[3] We therefore need to note that Ezekiel prophesied both before and after the second deportation in 586 B.C., when both the city and the temple of Jerusalem were destroyed.

Although we know very little about the life of the prophet, his ministry is characterized by the fact that, immediately after his calling, God silences the prophet so that he is not able to speak anymore (Ez 3:22–27). Additionally, God tells the prophet to stay in his house (v. 24). The muteness of the prophet continues until 586 B.C. when Babylonian troops finally break into the city (Ez 24:27; 33:21–22).

Moreover, Ezekiel was married and lost his wife roughly in 587 B.C., just before Nebuchadnezzar's troops capture Jerusalem (Ez 24:15–18).[4]

Finally, texts like Ez 8:1; 14:1; 20:1 and 33:30-31 describe how the elders of the exiled Jews sit before Ezekiel in order to receive the prophetic word from him. On the one hand, this points to Ezekiel's high authority for the exiled Jews: The elders of Israel, as the leading board of Israel, are submitting themselves to Ezekiel's ministry as the spiritual leader of Israel. This suggests the existence of the phenomenon of a school of the prophet Ezekiel. Zimmerli writes:

> "In all this, we cannot overlook the phenomenon of a 'school of the prophet', which edited the prophecies of Ezekiel, commented upon them, and gave them a fuller theo-

---

[3] William S. Lasor, "Ezekiel IX. Alternative Views and Additional Information," in *The International Standard Bible Encyclopedia 2*, ed. Geoffrey W. Brownlee et al. (Grand Rapids: Eerdmans, 1982), 262.

[4] Walther Zimmerli, *Ezekiel 1. A Commentary on the Book of the Prophet Ezekiel, Chapters 1–24*, Hermeneia, trans. R. E. Clements (Philadelphia: Fortress Press, 1979), 16.

> logical exposition. […] Undoubtedly, the present book of Ezekiel stems from the hand of the 'school'".[5]

2.2 The Vision Reports in the Book of Ezekiel

In this section some amount of preliminary information will be given in order to develop a basic understanding concerning the vision reports in the Book of Ezekiel. Scholars agree that the Book of Ezekiel contains four vision reports:

Vision 1:	Ez 1:1–3:15	Vision of the Glory of God (1:4-28) /
		Vision of the scroll (2:9-10)
Vision 2:	Ez 8:1–11:25	First vision of the temple
Vision 3:	Ez 37:1-14	Vision of the valley of dry bones
Vision 4:	Ez 40–48	Second vision of the Temple

The visions are interconnected in several ways: Every vision has some introductory verses with a precise date (see below p. 43ff., except for Ez 37:1-14), and describes how the *hand of Yahweh* came upon the prophet, (see p. 46ff.) and the actions of the spirit of Yahweh.

Besides that, Ez 8:4 (vision 2) refers back to Ez 1:28 and establishes a connection to vision 1. Ez 8:4 has "the glory of the God of Israel" and exactly that term appears in the closing verses of vision 1 (Ez 3:12, and also in 1:28, the last verse of the first part of the vision.

In Ez 37, in verses one and two, the word "valley" appears, thus establishing a connection back to Ez 8:4 (vision 2).

Ez 40–48 (vision 4) is connected to both Ez 1:4-28 (vision 1) and Ez 8–11 (vision 2). "And the vision I saw was just like the vision

---

[5] Zimmerli, *Ezekiel 1* (Hermeneia), 70-71.

that I had seen when he came to destroy the city [i.e. Ez 8–11, F.F.] and just like the vision that I had seen by the Chebar canal [i.e. Ez 1:4-28, F.F.]" (Ez 43:3).

Besides that, Ez 8–11 (vision 2) and Ez 40–48 (vision 4) are connected by their main topic, the temple. Just as the glory of Yahweh leaves the temple in Ez 10:4,18,19; 11:23, it comes back to re-enter the temple again in Ez 43:3-5.

Moreover, the first and the last visions of the Book of Ezekiel form an inclusio and provide a frame around the whole book. In his first vision (Ez 1:4-28) the prophet sees Yahweh sitting on a throne (Ez 1:26-28), and in the last vision Yahweh declares that the temple is "the place of my throne and the place of the soles of my feet" (Ez 43:7a). Note that the word "throne" represents power and in the given context it refers to Yahweh's reign as king.[6]

2.3 The Outline of the Book of Ezekiel

In order to get an orientation about the whole Book of Ezekiel, the four vision reports can provide clues to structure the book of Ezekiel.

It has oftentimes been observed that

> "the book of Ezekiel has two major components, a collection of units expressing a message of judgement (1:1–24:27) and a parallel collection offering a message of consolation (33:1–48:35). These are separated by a […] block of prophecies against foreign nations (25:1–32:32)".[7]

---

[6] Roland M. Hals, *Ezekiel*, Forms of Old Testament Literature 19 (Grand Rapids: Eerdmans, 1989), 3.

[7] Ibid.

The first part of the book announces the coming destruction of Jerusalem, while the last part presupposes the fall of Jerusalem.[8] Having said this, the structure of the book of Ezekiel is typical for a prophetic book with parallels found in the books of Isaiah (Is 1–39 announcing judgement and Is 40–66 consisting of prophecies of hope), Amos (Am 1:1–9:10 judgement / Am 9:11-15 promise of restoration) or Micah (Mi 1:2-2:11 judgement / Mi 2:12-13 salvation / Mi 3 judgement / Mi 4–5 salvation / Mi 6:1–7:6 judgement / Mi 7:7-20 salvation).

If we now consider the role of the visions, they provide a guide to a more detailed structure of the book:

Ez 1–3	**vision 1** Vision of the Glory of God (1:4-28)
	Vision of the scroll (2:9-10)
Ez 4–7	Words of judgement against Jerusalem
Ez 8–11	**vision 2** First vision of the temple (judgement)
Ez 12–24	Words of judgement against Jerusalem
Ez 25–32	Words of judgement against foreign nations
Ez 33–37	Words of consolation to Jerusalem
	vision 3 Vision of the valley of dry bones (37:1-14)
Ez 38–39	Gog from Magog
Ez 40–48	**vision 4** Second vision of the temple (consolation)

As we will see when we study the chronological details in chapter 4.1.1 (p. 43ff.) two of the four vision reports of the book were received before the destruction of Jerusalem (Ez 1–3 and 8–11) and two after the fall of Jerusalem (Ez 37:1-14 and 40–48).

---

[8] Hals, *Ezekiel* (FOTL 19), 3.

In addition, each vision fits well into the overall topic of the context: vision 1 (especially in 2:9-10) and vision 2 announce judgement (as in Ez 4–7 and 12–24), while visions 3 and 4 are meant as encouragement of Israel (as in 33–37 and 38–39; if we understand the fall of Israel's last enemy, Gog from Magog as good news for Jerusalem).

2.4 Ezekiel's Audience

As Ezekiel has been exiled into Babylon and is prophesying there, the question is to whom is Ezekiel directing his messages? Walter Zimmerli[9] differentiates three different recipients:

1. Ez 3:10-15 and 11:24-25 mention the *exiles* as specific addressees of Ezekiel's message. Remarkably, both texts are at the end of vision reports. Besides that, in 33:30-33 people from his immediate exilic environment appear.
2. Ezekiel addresses the *elders of Israel* in Ez 8:1; 14:1; 20:1.
3. Ez 11:14-21; 33:24-29 are addressed to those who remained in Palestine after the Babylonian deportations.

However, "in all this it is quite clear that Ezekiel in his preaching over and over again sees the people of God as a whole, no matter whether he is turning in particular to his exilic surroundings or is envisaging Jerusalem and Judah or is letting us hear the history of the nation as a whole".[10]

---

[9] Zimmerli, *Ezekiel 1* (Hermeneia), 55.

[10] Walther Zimmerli, *Ezekiel 2. A Commentary on the Book of the Prophet Ezekiel, Chapters 25–48*, Hermeneia, trans. James D. Martin (Philadelphia: Fortress Press, 1983), 564.

2.5 The Meaning of the Hebrew Root *r-'-h* (ראה)

Given the fact that every Hebrew word is characterized by its *root*, which usually consists of three consonants, the terms *ḥāzôn* and *maẖᵃzæh* belong to the same Hebrew root *ẖ-z-h* (חזה), while the third term *mar'æh* is derived from the root *r-'-h* (ראה).

As it is the aim of this study to cover all places in the Book of Ezekiel that have *nimit* in the Thai translation (THSV 2011), this study will have to address the question of whether there are other terms derived from *ẖ-z-h* or *r-'-h* that are translated by *nimit*. Also, the question is worth considering whether there are other roots besides *ẖ-z-h* or *r-'-h* that the Thai Bible translates with *nimit*.

Throughout the Old Testament the verb *r-'-h* appears 1,303 times. Additionally, nominal derivations of *r-'-h* occur 133 times.[11] This makes *r-'-h* one of the most frequently used roots in the Old Testament. Only six other roots count more appearances: אמר (*'-m-r* "say": 5305 times); היה (*h-y-h* "live": 3561 times); עשׂה (*'-s-h* "do": 2627 times); בוא (*b-w-'* "come": 2570 times); נתן (*n-t-n* "give": 2010 times) and הלךְ (*h-l-k* "go": 1547 times.[12]

In this section, I will give an overview over the multiple usages of *r-'-h*. The root denotes "seeing as a totality, in which sensation and perception merge. (…) The verb *rā'â* refers especially to that segment of the process that brings the perpetual flux of the visual experience of living reality to the level of conscious recognition".[13] When *r-'-h* appears together with "eye" it denotes the act of seeing

---

[11] Zimmerli, *Ezekiel 2* (Hermeneia), 23.

[12] Rüdiger Bartelmus, *Einführung in das Biblische Hebräisch, mit einem Anhang Biblisches Aramäisch* (Zürich: Theologischer Verlag, 2009), 233-235.

[13] Hans F. Fuhs, "רָאָה ra'ah," in *Theological Dictionary of the Old Testament* 13, ed. Johannes G. Botterweck, Helmer Ringgren and Heinz-Josef Fabry (Grand Rapids: William B. Eerdmans, 2004), 214.

something or somebody. Besides that, *r-'-h* often occurs in combination with "to hear" denoting the process of becoming aware of somebody or something.[14] *r-'-h* is also used for perception with other senses besides the sense of sight: "hear": Gn 2:19; 42:1; "feel", "sense": Is 44:16 (heat); "enjoy": Eccl 8:16 (sleep); 9:9 (life); "encounter": Jer 5:12 (war, famine); Jb 7:7 (good things); Ps 89:49 (death).[15]

Additionally, according to Vetter,[16] several figurative meanings have developed from the main meaning of *r-'-h*. In some cases, the root denotes the act of mental perception ("discover", "realize", "become aware of"; Gn 16:4f.; 1 Sam 26:12; Is 29:15). In addition, *r-'-h* is used for general expressions of human life, like "*to see the light*" = "to live" (Jb 33:28; Eccl 7:11; Ps 49:20) or "*to see the face of*" = "*to associate with*" in 2 Kgs 25:19. When in an intensive sense, *r-'-h* means "*to look after*", "*to take care of*" (Jb 37:24; Gn 39:23) and "*to select*" or "*to choose*" (Gn 41:33; 1 Sam 16:17).

When *r-'-h* is used theologically, it stands for the act of seeing God or his face (Gn 32:31; Jgs 6:22). Also, several attributes of God can be the object of *r-'-h*: God's friendliness (Ps 27:4), his power and majesty (Ps 63:3).

Oftentimes, God is the subject of *r-'-h*: Whenever God turns toward Israel in order to help them out of their hardships, God is said to see the distress of Israel or of a single Israelite (Ex 3:7-8; Ps 35:17).[17] *r-'-h* expresses God's affection and care towards Israel. In this respect, *r-'-h* also appears to denote that Israel (or one Israelite)

---

[14] Fuhs, "רָאָה ra'ah," (TDOT 13), 216.

[15] D. Vetter, "ראה r'h sehen," in *Theologisches Handwörterbuch zum Alten Testament* 2, ed. Ernst Jenni and Claus Westermann (Gütersloh: Chr. Kaiser / Gütersloher Verlagshaus, [6]2004), 693.

[16] Ibid., 693f.

[17] Ibid., 697.

"experiences" (="sees") God's intervention and his help (Ex 34:10; Dt 3:21; Is 42:18.20).

More important for this study is the observation that *r-'-h* denotes the occurrence of a vision and usually includes hearing as well.[18] Vetter also notes that the root *r-'-h* belongs to the typical language of a vision report.[19] The feminine term *mar'â* stands for the visionary event in itself, whereby the masculine noun *mar'ê* can be used likewise.[20]

Finally, *r-'-h* is used in the niph'al stem, when God (Gn 17:1; Ex 3:2), his glory (Ex 16:10; Nm 14:10) or his Angel appear.[21]

2.6 The Meaning of the Hebrew Root *ḥ-z-h* (חזה)

The root חזה (*ḥ-z-h*) is an Aramaic loanword in Hebrew and has a wide range of meanings. It can refer to the natural vision of the eyes as well as to supernatural, unusual experiences of seeing. Generally speaking it holds a similar position as its Hebrew counterpart ראה.

Statistically, there are 115 passages that have a form of *ḥ-z-h* throughout the Old Testament; of these, 86 are in prophetic texts (14 in Ezekiel). This particular association might come from the fact that derivatives of *ḥ-z-h* are frequently associated with *nābî'* ("prophet").

"What is meant, when *chāzāh*, *chāzôn*, or *chizzāyôn* is used in connection with a nabi? (…) The answer is unambiguous: not a visual image but a word from God. (…) According to Ps 89:20(19), God

---

[18] Vetter, "ראה r'h sehen" (THAT 2), 697.

[19] Ibid.

[20] Ibid., 699.

[21] Ibid., 700-701.

spoke in a *chāzôn*; a *chāzôn* is thus an event in which words are received."[22]

> "Thus for *chāzāh*, etc., in the context of the nabis, we may conclude that it refers to a revelation of the divine word, usually at night during a (deep) sleep and sometimes associated with emotional agitation. Visual manifestation, however, plays no role, or at most a minor one."[23]

In summary, the Aramaic root *ḥ-z-h* was in use despite the fact that there was a Hebrew word for seeing (*r-'-h*), because it was a "technical term for a particular nocturnal experience of the divine word, distinct from dreams".[24] Jepsen, however, notes that in the later period all the special associations of *chāzôn* seem to have vanished, so that Dn 8 and Dn 10 do not distinguish between *chāzôn* and *mar'ê.*[25]

If we leave the prophetic context, the root *ḥ-z-h* is used when non-prophets are seeing God, like the elders of Israel in Ex 24:11 or Jb (19:26-27) – but this applies only to the late period.[26] In another non-prophetic sense, the root *ḥ-z-h* is used for inspecting something: In this sense, God is inspecting men (Ps 11:4; 17:2) and Moses is advised to "Choose able men from all the people" (Ex 18:21).[27]

---

[22] Alfred Jepsen, "חָזָה chāzāh," in *Theological Dictionary of the Old Testament* 4, ed. Johannes G. Botterweck, Helmer Ringgren and Heinz-Josef Fabry (Grand Rapids: William B. Eerdmans, 1980), 283.

[23] Ibid., 284.

[24] Ibid., 285.

[25] Ibid., 288.

[26] Ibid., 288-289.

[27] Ibid., 289.

2.7 Excursus: The Use of *ḥ-z-h* (חזה) in Superscriptions

The interim result that *ḥ-z-h* means the revelation of a word of God and not of an image, is verified and highlighted by the use of *ḥ-z-h* in the superscriptions of some prophetic books in the Old Testament.

> *Is 1:1* The vision (*ḥāzôn*) of Isaiah the son of Amoz, which he saw (*ḥāzâ*) concerning Judah and Jerusalem.
>
> *Is 2:1* The word (*haddābār*) that Isaiah the son of Amoz saw (*ḥāzâ*).
>
> *Is 13:1* The oracle (*maśśā'*) concerning Babylon which Isaiah the son of Amoz saw (ḥāzâ).
>
> *Am 1:1* The words (*dibrê*) of Amos, who was among the shepherds of Tekoa, which he saw (*ḥāzâ*) concerning Israel.
>
> *Ob 1* The vision (*ḥāzôn*) of Obadiah.
>
> *Mi 1:1* The word (*dābār*) of the Lord that came to Micah of Moresheth … which he saw (*ḥāzâ*) concerning Samaria and Jerusalem.
>
> *Na 1:1* An oracle (*maśśā'*) concerning Nineveh. The book of the vision (*ḥāzôn*) of Nahum of Elkosh.
>
> *Hb 1:1* The oracle (*maśśā'*) that Habakkuk the prophet saw (*ḥāzâ*).

The word *maśśā'* that is found in the superscriptions of Is 13:1; Na 1:1 and Hb 1:1, is derived from the Hebrew root *n-ś-h* that means "to lift up" or to "raise". *maśśā'* is a noun derived from this root and means the process by which someone lifts up his or her voice in order to speak; thus "utterance" would be a suitable translation for *maśśā* in the contexts above.[28]

[28] Hans-Peter Müller, "מַשָּׂא maśśā'," *in Theological Dictionary of the Old Testament 9*, ed. Johannes G. Botterweck, Helmer Ringgren and

In the superscriptions above, the prophet often "*ḥāzâ*"s a *maśśā*, which can only mean that the prophet has received a spoken message from Yahweh. Yet other cases are even clearer: The prophet has *ḥāzâ*ed a *dābār* of Yahweh, a word of God.

The headlines of prophetic books thus underline the meaning of *ḥāzâ* and its derivatives: They are used when the prophet receives a spoken word of God.

Heinz-Joseph Fabry (Grand Rapids: William B. Eerdmans, 1998), 22-24.

3 *ḥāzôn*, *mar'ê* and *maḥăzê* in the Book of Ezekiel

As it is the aim of the current study to analyze the use of the term นิมิต (*nimit*) as an equivalent for the Hebrew words חָזוֹן (*ḥāzôn*), מַרְאֶה (*mar'ê*), and מַחֲזֶה (*maḥăzê*), this chapter has been outlined as follows: First of all, I will describe the use of each word in the Book of Ezekiel in detail. Having finished that task, the background and the meaning of these three words will be explained. After that, the use of *nimit* for these three words will be studied in order to find out if the translation is consistent or if there are any abnormalities in the use of *nimit* for *ḥazon*, *mar'ê,* and *maḥze* in the Book of Ezekiel.

3.1 *ḥāzôn* (חָזוֹן) in the Book of Ezekiel

3.1.1 Occurrence

The term *ḥāzôn* appears seven times in the Book of Ezekiel and *only outside the four vision reports* in the Book of Ezekiel: Ez 7:13,26; 12:22,23,24,27; 13:16.

3.1.2 Meaning

According to Jepsen, the term *ḥāzôn*

> "refers to a special type of divine revelation, probably during the night but distinct from a dream. In any case, it is assumed that the God of Israel makes use of this method to reveal his word, just as he uses dreams and Urim (1 Sam 28:6). Above all, the word of God as revealed to the nabis (= prophets, F.F.) through *chāzôn*".[1]

---

[1] Jepsen, "חָזָה chāzāh" (TDOT 4), 290.

3.1.3 The Use of nimit *in the Thai Translation of* ḥāzôn

The use of *nimit* in the Thai translation of the Hebrew term *ḥāzôn* is described in Table 1 in the appendix (see p. 101).

- In all cases, where Hebrew has *ḥāzôn*, the Thai Bible (TSV 2011), has *nimit*. The use of this Thai term as translation for *ḥāzôn* is consistent.
- *Ḥāzôn* is only one term among others (e.g. *mar'ê, mar'â, maḥăzê*), which is translated as *nimit*. As Bible readers are usually not aware of the fact that there are several Hebrew words involved, for them, the Bible text does not differentiate between those terms at all. However, as already set out in chapter 2, there is a huge difference between *ḥāzôn* and *mar'ê* / *mar'â*.
- In Ez 7:26 *ḥāzôn* is clearly "an event in which words are received".[2] This is obvious from the fact that v. 26b consists of three parts: Next to the *ḥāzôn*, law, and counsel from the elders are mentioned; all three have in common that words are spoken, when *ḥāzôn*, law, or counsel are passed on from God to the prophet or from one person to another.
- It is striking though that most of the occurrences are found in Ez 12, to be more precise in the section Ez 12:21–28. In this section, there are two indicators that mark out this section against the context:

  (1) V. 21 has the formula "And the word of the LORD came to me" which introduces a new section of text. As this sentence occurs again in v. 26, we consider v. 21–25 and v. 26–28 as two subsections of v. 21–28.

  (2) Both in v. 22 and in v. 23 the prophet picks up a saying that goes around among the people of Israel. They deal with the fact that a *ḥāzôn* that a prophet has spoken is delayed before it

---

[2] Jepsen, "חָזָה chāzāh" (TDOT 4), 283.

is fulfilled. According to God's word to the prophet, all the *ḥāzôn* that God has given will come true without delay (v. 23,25,28). Besides that, there will be no more false *ḥāzôn* in the future (v. 24).

Another observation in Ez 12:21-25,26-28 is that *ḥāzôn* and *dābār* ("word") seem to be used interchangeably: While the people say that the *ḥāzôn* (v. 22,27) will be delayed, God says that the fulfilment of his word (*dābār,* v. 25,28) will not be delayed. Moreover, v. 23b is to be rendered as "The days are near, and the word (*dābār*) of every vision (*ḥāzôn*)."[3] This is one more hint that a *ḥāzôn* consists of the revelation of a word of God.

The section Ez 12:21-25,26-28 also touches the topic of false prophecy (v. 24) and anticipates the topic of the following verses in Ez 13.

3.2 *mar'ê* (מַרְאֶה) in the Book of Ezekiel

3.2.1 Occurrence

The term *mar'ê* occurs 36 times and in 20 verses in the Book of Ezekiel (Ez 1:5,13,14,16,26,27,28; 8:2,4; 10:1,9,10,22; 11:24; 23:15,16; 40:3; 41:21; 42:11; 43:3); for the following compare Table 2 in the appendix (p. 101ff.).

The distribution of the term among the chapters is notable and therefore deserves a closer look. Scholars generally agree that the Book of Ezekiel contains visionary reports in chapters 1–3 (vision 1); 8–11 (vision 2); 37:1–14 (vision 3) and 40–48 (vision 4). This means that 34 out of 36 occurrences of *mar'ê* are found in the vision reports of the Book of Ezekiel, while only 2 occurrences (Ez 23:15,16) are not found in visionary reports.

---

[3] Zimmerli, *Ezekiel 1* (Hermeneia), 274.

Another observation is important: *mar'ê* seems to be used frequently in the beginning and closing sections of a visionary report.

- In vision 1 of the book (Ez 1–3), we have *mar'ê* in 1:5, then in v. 13, 14, 16, and then again in v. 26–28, the latter verses being the closing part of a subsection of Ez 1–3: In v. 28 the vision of the throne of God and its surroundings comes to an end and in 2:1 God starts to talk to the prophet.[4]
- In vision 2 (Ez 8–11) of the book, *mar'ê* is found in the opening section (8:2-4, *mar'ê* in v. 2 and 4) and in the closing section of the report (11:22-25, *mar'ê* in v. 24). The third vision report (Ez 37:1-14) does not have *mar'ê*.
- Vision 4 (Ez 40–48) also has *mar'ê* in the opening section (*mar'ê* in 40:3).

3.2.2 Meaning

Morphologically, the Hebrew term מַרְאֶה consists of the root *r-'-h*, (ראה) and the prefix *m* (מ). According to Fuhs, *mar'ê* can be translated in three different ways, depending on the context in which the word is used.

3.2.2.1 Everyday Usage

"*mar'eh* denotes the act of seeing (with one's eyes: Lev. 13:12; Dt. 28:34,67; Josh 22:10; Isa. 11:3 [outward appearance]; Ez 23:15-16), appearance (Gn 39:6; 1 Sam 17:42; etc.), and bearing (Cant. 2:14; 5:15)".[5] If we turn to the Book of Ezekiel, the only two occurrences of *mar'ê* outside the vision reports (Ez 23:15,16) are to

[4] Achim Behrens, *Prophetische Visionsschilderungen im Alten Testament: Sprachliche Eigenarten, Funktion und Geschichte einer Gattung,* Alter Orient und Altes Testament 292 (Münster: Ugarit-Verlag, 2002), 185.

[5] Fuhs, "רָאָה ra'ah" (TDOT 13), 208-242, 240.

be understood in this sense: In v. 15, the Babylonian men have an appearance (*mar'ê*) like chariot officers (NIV) and in v. 16 Oholibah (Jerusalem) lusts after them, as soon as they appear (*mar'ê*) before her eyes. Having said this, I will now turn to the rest of the occurrences of *mar'ê*, all of them in the visionary reports of the book of Ezekiel.

3.2.2.2 "Vision"

mar'ê is also used when the prophet wants to express that he has received a vision from God. This is the case only in Ez 11:24 and 43:3.[6]

> *Ez 11:24* And the Spirit lifted me up and brought me in the vision (*mar'ê*) by the Spirit of God into Chaldea, to the exiles. Then the vision (*mar'ê*) that I had seen went up from me.

> *Ez 43:3* And the vision (*mar'ê*) that I saw was like the vision (*mar'ê*) that I had seen when he came to destroy the city, and just like the vision (*mar'ê* plural) that I had seen by the Chebar Canal.

3.2.2.3 "Appearance"

In all the other cases, the term *mar'ê* is used to describe the *appearance* of things and entities the prophet sees in a vision. As the prophet is a human being who is not able to fully understand and describe what he sees in visions, the prophet makes use of the Hebrew preposition כְּ (*kĕ* "like") very often:

> *Ez 1:14* And the living creatures darted to and fro, *like the appearance* (*kĕmar'ê*) of a flash of lightning.

---

[6] Fuhs, "רָאָה ra'ah" (TDOT 13), 239.

Ez 1:28 Like the appearance (*kĕmar'ê*) of the bow that is in the cloud on the day of rain, so was the radiance of the brightness all around.

Ez 40:3a When he brought me there, behold, there was a man whose appearance (*mar'ê*) was like (*kĕmar'ê* "the appearance of") bronze.

The last example given above actually uses the reduplication of *mar'ê* and has *mar'ê kĕmar'ê* ("the appearance of … was like the appearance of …", FF). This structure is also found in Ez 41:21 and 43:3.

3.2.3 The Use of nimit *in the Thai Translation of* mar'ê

In the following section I will analyze in which places the Thai word *nimit* is used in translating *mar'ê* in the Book of Ezekiel and which other words are used in the translation (THSV 2011).

The following observations are striking when studying the occurrences of *mar'ê* and *nimit*:

- As already mentioned, *mar'ê* appears almost exclusively in the visionary reports of the book (Ez 1–3, 8–11, 37:1–14 and 40–48), Ez 23:15,16 being the only exceptions. In these two cases (Ez 23:15.16) *mar'ê* appears in everyday usage (see above 3.2.2.1).
- In most cases, *mar'ê* is translated by the term ลักษณะ, (*laksana*) and the Hebrew preposition כְּ (*kĕ* "like") that often accompanies *mar'ê*, is translated by เหมือน (*muean*) or คล้าย (*khlay*) – both words mean "like". These are the cases where the English renders *mar'ê* as "appearance" (see above 3.2.2.3).
- In Ez 8:4 the Thai Standard Version of 2011 continues to use *laksana*, but adds the royal language prefix พระ (*phra*), as this verse is about the appearance of God's glory. *Phra* is a Thai prefix denoting the royal or divine nature of something or

somebody. The Thai Standard Version of 1971 however, translated *mar'ê* as นิมิต (*nimit*).

- The other verses that use *nimit* ("vision", see above 3.2.2.2) to translate *mar'ê* are Ez 11:24 and 43:3. In both verses *mar'ê* is followed by the relative clause *ăšer rā'îtî* ("that I had seen": 8:4; 11:24b; 43:3 [3x]): "the vision that I had seen". As Ez 8:4 uses this wording as well, the rendering of *mar'ê* as *nimit* in Ez 8:4 seems to fit better. In all these verses (including 8:4), *mar'ê* has the Hebrew article (thus *hammar'ê*).
- The fact that Ez 43:3 has four forms of *mar'ê* and one form of *mar'â*, has led some exegetes to the impression that the text is overloaded.[7] The details of this verse will be discussed in Appendix 2 (p. 106f.).

To summarize, there are three verses altogether in the Book of Ezekiel, where *mar'ê* is translated as *nimit* (Ez 8:4; 11:24 and 43:3, highlighted in grey in the table (see Appendix 1, p. 101ff.). In these cases, *mar'ê* carries the article and is often followed by "that I had seen". Most of the verses in the Book of Ezekiel with *mar'ê* however, translate it with *laksana*.

3.3 *maḥăzê* (מַחֲזֵה) in the Book of Ezekiel

Another term which is also derived from the same Hebrew root as *ḥāzôn* is the word *maḥăzê*. It occurs only in Ez 13:7a: "Have you not seen (*ḥăzîtem*) a false vision (*maḥăzê*)?"

This verse combines the verb *ḥāzâ* and the noun *maḥăzê,* derived from the same root (*ḥ-z-h*). That this verse speaks of false visions relates back to Ez 12:21-25,26-28 (see above p. 33f.), which deals with the same topic (v. 24). In Ez 13:7b however, the prophet em-

[7] Zimmerli, *Ezekiel 2* (Hermeneia) 407; Leslie C. Allen, *Ezekiel 20–48,* Word Biblical Commentary 29 (Dallas: Word Books, 1990), 242.

phasizes that Yahweh has not *spoken* what the false prophets have received (*wa'ănî lō' dibbartî*). Besides that, the term *nĕ'um* is frequently used as a "formula for an utterance of Yahweh" that "means simply 'speak'" and is often found "in parallel or variation with → דבר *dābhār*".[8] This clearly indicates, that *maḥăzê* is about spoken words.

The next two sections will cover two more words besides *ḥāzôn*, *mar'ê* and *maḥăzê*, that are also translated as *nimit* in the THSV 2011: The noun *mar'â* (מַרְאָה) and the verb *ḥāzâ* (חָזָה). By doing so, all occurrences of *nimit* in the THSV 2011 will be covered.

3.4 *mar'â* (מַרְאָה) in the Book of Ezekiel

3.4.1 Occurrence

With only four occurrences in the Book of Ezekiel, the term *mar'â* occurs less often than *mar'ê*: Ez 1:1; 8:3; 40:2; 43:3.

3.4.2 Meaning

According to Fuhs, the "noun *mar'â*, usually in the plural, denotes the occurrences of a visionary event (Num 12:6 par. *ḥ^a^lôm*; in 1 Sam 3:15 it refers to an auditory event)."[9]

---

[8] Hermann Eising, "נְאֻם ne'um," in *Theological Dictionary of the Old Testament* 9, ed. Johannes G. Botterweck, Helmer Ringgren and Heinz-Josef Fabry (Grand Rapids: William B. Eerdmans, 1998), 110 (e.g. Jer 23:31; Ez 37:14; Zech 12:1; Pr 30:1).

[9] Fuhs, "רָאָה ra'ah" (TDOT 13), 239.

3.4.3 The Use of nimit *in the Thai Translation of* mar'â

After compiling the uses of both *mar'â* and *nimit* in the Hebrew Bible (see Table 3 in the appendix, p. 104f.) and in the Thai translation, the following points are striking:

- The Book of Ezekiel uses only *mar'ôt*, which is the plural of *mar'â*.
- In three of the four cases, *mar'ôt* is connected with the Hebrew term *'ĕlōhîm* (Ez 1:1; 8:3; 40:2). The question that follows from this observation is whether *'ĕlōhîm* is an objective genitive or a subjective genitive: Is God the *object* in a sense that Ezekiel is seeing God (objective genitive) or are the visions created and given *by God* (subjective genitive)? Besides that, one also has to consider that *'ĕlōhîm* could be translated as something other than "God" in the sense of Yahweh.

  The term *'ĕlōhîm* is an appellative that denotes "superhuman beings including God and angels".[10] According to Michael Heiser, the word is used for six different entities in the unseen realm: Yahweh, the God of Israel (Gn 2:4-5; Dt 4:35), members of Yahweh's heavenly council (Ps 82:1,6), Gods and goddesses of other nations (Jgs 11:24; 1 Kgs 11:33), Demons (Dt 32:17), the deceased Samuel (1 Sam 28:13), Angels or the Angel of Yahweh (Gen 35:7).[11] "What all the figures on the list have in common is that they are inhabitants of the spiritual world."[12]

---

[10] Francis Brown, S. R. Driver and Charles A. Briggs (eds.), *Hebrew and English Lexikon of the Old Testament (*Oxford: Clarendon Press, 1974), 43.

[11] Michael Heiser, *The Unseen Realm. Recovering the Supernatural Worldview of the Bible* (Bellingham: Lexham Press, 2015), 31.

[12] Ibid., 32.

It is not impossible to understand *'ĕlōhîm* as subjective genitive, if one takes *'ĕlōhîm* as Yahweh, who lets Ezekiel see a vision. Block, however, affirms the fact that *'ĕlōhîm* is used as an appellative here and takes the term as objective genitive; mar'ôt is a plural of generalization.[13] In his translation "divine vision"[14] however, *'ĕlōhîm* seems to be used as an attributive genitive.[15] It seems better to really understand *'ĕlōhîm* as objective genitive: This fits well to the fact that in his vision, Ezekiel sees all kinds of divine beings: Yahweh, Cherubim, living beings around the throne and even *divine places and realities*, like the throne of Yahweh.[16]

3.5 Other Verses with *nimit* in Ezekiel

Finally, in order to make sure that this study covers all occurrences of *nimit* in the TSV 2011, this final section considers all the verses that have *nimit* in the Thai translation, but none of *mar'ê*, *mar'â*, *ḥāzôn* and *maḥăzê*: Ez 13:6–9, 23; 21:29; 22:28 (see Table 4 in the appendix, p. 105f.). Interestingly, these verses do not have another *noun* which is derived from the Hebrew root *ḥ-z-h*, but they all have the *verb ḥāzâ*.

– Four out of six places, where the THSV 2011 has *nimit* and Hebrew has the verb *ḥāzâ* are found in Ez 13. This chapter deals with false prophets, and it is therefore not surprising, that

[13] Daniel I. Block, *The Book of Ezekiel: Chapters 1–24*. New International Commentary of the Old Testament (Grand Rapids: Eerdmans, 1997), 85.

[14] Ibid.

[15] Daniel B. Wallace, *Greek Grammar Beyond the Basics. An Exegetical Syntax of the New Testament* (Grand Rapids: Zondervan, 1996), 86-88.

[16] Block, *The Book of Ezekiel: Chapters 1–24* (NICOT), 85.

šāw' (“emptiness”)[17] occurs in almost all places (Ez 13:6,9,23); Ez 13:8 also has *šāw'*, but not as direct object of *ḥāzâ*. ESV translates “to see false visions” in Ez 13:6,9,23. Allen[18] points out that the word emptiness is used to express that the announcements of the false prophets did not come true.

- It is difficult to decide if *ḥāzâ* refers more *to see*[ing] a vision or to receive a word from God, as it usually is the case with *ḥāzâ*. At the very least we can be sure that what the false prophets have seen, or heard, is not from God, as he has neither sent them (Ez 13:6) nor spoken to them (Ez 13:7). However, as v. 7 has “I [the Lord] have not spoken” it seems as if *ḥāzâ* is more connected to false prophets receiving spoken messages then seeing something. Ez 22:28 also points towards this point of view: In the end, the false prophets announce: “Thus says the Lord”, no matter if they have seen or heard a message from somewhere, but surely not from God.
- Ez 21:29 is dealing with false prophecy among the Ammonites.

3.6 Interim Summary

The noun *ḥāzôn* occurs seven times in the Book of Ezekiel and it is *never* used in the vision reports of the Book (Ez 1–3; 8–11; 37:1-14; 40–48): All seven verses with *ḥāzôn* are found in non-visionary texts. The Thai Bible (THSV 2011) translates *ḥāzôn* consistently as *nimit* in all cases, although the Hebrew root (*ḥ-z-h*) refers more *to receiving a word that God has spoken* than to seeing God’s message in images and symbols.

---

[17] Brown / Driver / Briggs (eds.), *Hebrew and English Lexikon*, 996.

[18] Leslie C. Allen, *Ezekiel 1–19,* Word Biblical Commentary 28 (Dallas: Word Books, 1994), 201.

In contrast to *ḥāzôn*, the term *mar'ê* appears more often in Ezekiel. Almost all of the 36 occurrences are to be found in the visionary texts of the book; Ez 23:15,16 being the only exceptions. The Hebrew preposition *kĕ* which often accompanies *mar'ê* in 17 out of 36 cases is rendered as *muean* or *khlay* ("like"). As it has been the case with *ḥāzôn*, the translation into Thai is consistent as follows:

- In most of the cases (30 times), *mar'ê* does not have the article, and is translated by *laksana* ("appearance").
- When *mar'ê* does have the article however (6 times), it is five times followed by a relative clause "that I saw" and it is usually translated as *nimit* in TSV 2011. This is the case in Ez 11:24b and 43:3 (3x).
- In Ez 8:4 *mar'ê* has both the article and the relative clause. The Thai Standard Version of 2011 has *laksana*, but, on the other hand, the Thai Standard Version of 1971 has *nimit*, which is to be preferred.

The word *maḥăzê* appears only once in the Book of Ezekiel (Ez 13:7). As the context of this verse (Ez 12:21-25+26-28) has *ḥāzôn* four times and as *ḥāzôn* and *maḥăzê* have the same Hebrew root (*ḥ-z-h*), it seems very likely that *maḥăzê* here means the receiving of a word of God, like *ḥāzôn*. The Thai translation is *nimit*.

Besides *ḥāzôn*, *mar'ê,* and *maḥăzê*, there is one more word, *mar'â*, which is translated with *nimit*. It appears four times only in its plural form *mar'ôt* and the Thai (THSV 1971 and THSV 2011) have *nimit* (Ez 1:1; 8:3; 40:2) or do not translate *mar'ôt* (Ez 43:3).

All the other occurrences of *nimit* have the verb *ḥāzâ*, and refer to a revelation of the word of Yahweh.

Having given this summary, two of the objectives of the present study (see above p. 14) have already been achieved: (1) "To clarify the meaning of the terms *ḥāzôn*, *mar'ê,* and *maḥăzê* in the Book of Ezekiel." And (2) "To study the use of the Thai word *nimit* in translating *ḥāzôn*, *mar'ê,* and *maḥăzê*."

4 The Meaning of the Visions on the Book of Ezekiel

This chapter contains a detailed study of the concepts that are behind חָזוֹן (*ḥāzôn*) / מַחֲזֶה (*maḥăzê*) / חָזָה (*ḥāzâ*) and מַרְאֶה (*mar'ê*) / מַרְאָה (*mar'â*). In order to define these concepts, it is not enough to only search the meaning, translation, and occurrence of words; an analysis of the content of the visions is necessary. After that, having gained a proper understanding of the visions in the Book of Ezekiel and the concepts behind them, ideas that will help the Thai Christians to understand the visions of Ezekiel can be developed in chapter 5.

4.1 Introductions and Closing Sections of the Vision Reports

If one reads the text carefully, one will soon recognize that the four vision reports in the Book of Ezekiel have some verses as an introduction and in addition to that, some verses as a conclusion. The introductions to the visionary reports contain important details concerning the date and the process of receiving the visions. I will therefore start working on those introductory and closing verses in order to understand what happened when Ezekiel received a vision and to discover the concepts behind the visionary texts.

	Introduction	Conclusion
Vision 1 (Ez 1:1–3:15)	Ez 1:1-3	Ez 3:12-15
Vision 2 (Ez 8:1–11:25)	Ez 8:1-3	Ez 11:24-25
Vision 3 (Ez 37:1-14)	Ez 37:1	---
Vision 4 (Ez 40–48)	Ez 40:1-4	---

4.1.1 The Dating of the Vision Reports

That the vision reports give the exact date when each vision was received by the prophet is quite unique in the Bible. Usually dates in biblical texts are to be found only in the heading of the whole book. In addition, those verses usually only describe under which king of Israel or Judah this particular prophet served:

> *Am 1:1* The words of Amos, who was among the shepherds of Tekoa, which he saw concerning Israel *in the days of Uzziah king of Judah and in the days of Jeroboam the son of Joash, king of Israel*, two years before the earthquake.
>
> *Is 1:1* The vision of Isaiah the son of Amoz, which he saw concerning Judah and Jerusalem *in the days of Uzziah, Jotham, Ahaz, and Hezekiah, kings of Judah.*

Other prophetic books (if they have headlines giving dates) make use of the same pattern. Ezekiel differs from them, as he gives the exact day, month, and year of the time when he received a vision. Besides Ezekiel, only Haggai and Zechariah give the exact dates of the revelations they received (Hg 1:1,15; 2:1; 2:10,20 and Zec 1:1; 1:7; 7:1).

However, the dates in the Book of Ezekiel all refer back to 592 B.C., the year when king Jehoiachin was exiled (2 Kgs 24:10–16). The reason why Ezekiel refers back to Jehoiachin is most probably to be found in the fact that the Judeans did not accept Jehoiachin's followers (Zedekiah and Gedaliah), as they were imposed on Judah by Nebuchadnezzar (see 2 Kgs 24:17 and 25:22).

The dates in the vision reports of the book of Ezekiel are to be found in Ez 1:1; 8:1 and in 40:1 as follows:

First deportation of Jews to Babylon		597 B.C.
Vision 1	year 5[1], month 4, day 5 (Ez 1:1f.)	July 31, 593[2]
Vision 2	year 6, month 6, day 5 (Ez 8:1)	Sept. 18, 592

[1] Block, *The Book of Ezekiel: Chapters 1–24* (NICOT), 82.

[2] Ibid., 87; the "30th year" of Ez 1:1 might refer to the age of the prophet.

Second deportation of Jews to Babylon / destruction of Jerusalem		587
Vision 3	*no date*	*no date*
Vision 4	year 25, month 1, day 10 (Ez 40:1)	Apr. 28, 573

From all the given dates, the first two (Ez 1:1–2 and Ez 8:1) relate to revelations in a time between the first exile, in which both Jehoiachin and Ezekiel were exiled (597 B.C.), and the second exile, in which Jerusalem was destroyed (586 B.C.). Only the third one (Ez 40:1) refers to a time after Jerusalem was already struck down. Later, when we examine the content of the visions, it will appear that the vision recorded in Ez 8–11 contains a revelation concerning the fall of Jerusalem, which happened five years after the revelation. We can therefore say that at least this vision anticipates things that will happen in the future. But is that true for the other visions as well?

4.1.2 The "Opening of the Heavens" (Ez 1:1)

> *Ez 1:1* In the thirtieth year, in the fourth month, on the fifth day of the month, as I was among the exiles by the Chebar canal, *the heavens were opened*, and I saw visions of God.

Even though Ezekiel has the "opening of the heavens" (*niptĕḥû haššāmayim*) only in Ez 1:1, this motif is found both inside and outside Old Testament literature (2 Bar 22:1; Test Levi 2:6; 5:1; 18:6; 3 Macc 6:18; Mt 3:16; Rev 4:1; 19,1) and also in Acts 7:56. Mal 3:10 ("if I will not open the windows of heaven for you") comes close to that.

Within the three-level worldview of the Ancient Near East, which includes the heavens, the earth, and the underworld, *šāmayim* means the sphere of God presented as a vast space and, more specifically, the place of residence of God. K.-F. Pohlmann explains that the opening of the sky, which here marks the threshold to transcendence, means that Yahweh grants the prophet insight into higher spheres. At the same time, the divine visions enable the prophet to perceive a 'meta-level' above or beyond reality.[3]

The expression of the "opening of the heavens" in Ez 1:1 means that Ezekiel gets access to the transcendent world of God and divine beings. He is able to look into the heavenly world and into the heavenly throne room of God.[4] If, however, the barrier between the heavenly and the earthly reality breaks down, the Prophet comes more strongly into Yahweh's sphere of influence than ever before. Therefore, it is not surprising that the *coming of Yahweh's hand* initiates all the visionary accounts of the Book of Ezekiel (Ez 1:3b; 8:1; 37:1; 40:1).

4.1.3 The "Hand of Yahweh"

It is very striking that the expression "hand of God" (*yad yhwh*) appears frequently in the introductions and conclusions of the vision reports in the book of Ezekiel.

Vision 1 (1:3)	"the *hand of the LORD* was upon him"
(3:14)	"the *hand of the LORD* being strong upon me"
Vision 2 (8:1)	"the *hand of the Lord GOD* fell upon me"
Vision 3 (37:1)	"the *hand of the LORD* was upon me"
Vision 4 (40:1)	"the *hand of the LORD* was upon me"

Interestingly, the coming or falling of the "hand of Yahweh" precedes every single vision report in the Book of Ezekiel. This means that the "hand of Yahweh" seems to be a precondition that is neces-

---

[3] Pohlmann, Karl-F. *Das Buch des Propheten Hesekiel (Ezechiel) Kapitel 1-19 übersetzt und erklärt.* Altes Testament Deutsch 22/1. Göttingen: Vandenhoeck & Ruprecht, 1996, 61.

[4] Cooper, Lamar E. *Ezekiel.* The New American Commentary 17. Nashville: B&H Books, 1994, 60.

sary and that enables Ezekiel to receive the visionary revelation. According to Daniel L. Block, the expression "hand of God" refers to "the overwhelming pressure that God exerts on the prophet. In this prophet's ministry Yahweh's 'hand' exercises complete control over his movements, even transporting him back and forth to distant places".[5] When receiving a vision, Ezekiel is totally under the power of Yahweh.

4.1.4 Transporting of the Prophet

Not only is Ezekiel able to gaze into the heavenly sphere and is under the power of Yahweh, Ezekiel is also transported to a different place.

As already set out above, Ezekiel has been living among the exiles in Babylon (Ez 1:1). However, the Book of Ezekiel reports that the prophet is transported to a different place.

4.1.4.1 Ez 3:12–15

> 12 *Then the Spirit lifted me up*, and I heard behind me the voice of a great earthquake: "Blessed be the glory of the LORD from its place!" 13 It was the sound of the wings of the living creatures as they touched one another, and the sound of the wheels beside them, and the sound of a great earthquake. 14 *The Spirit lifted me up and took me away*, and I went in bitterness in the heat of my spirit, the hand of the LORD being strong upon me. 15 *And I came to the exiles at Tel-abib*, who were dwelling by the Chebar canal, and I sat where they were dwelling. And I sat there overwhelmed among them seven days.

This text forms the closing section of the vision report Ez 1–3. When the prophet started to receive the vision in Ez 1:1-3 it did not seem as if he was being brought to another place; the text makes no

---

[5] Block, *The Book of Ezekiel: Chapters 1–24* (NICOT), 89.

mention of such a process. But now, as the visionary experience comes to an end, the spirit lifts Ezekiel up (v. 12), takes him away (v. 14) and finally Ezekiel comes to the exiles in Babylon (v. 15).

Quite contrary to the introductory section (where he does not explain clearly how, or if, he entered the unseen world), Ezekiel reports how he comes back and re-enters the world he used to know. "The supernatural journey ends at his exilic settlement, which was evidently some distance away from the scene of the vision", writes Leslie C. Allen.[6]

4.1.4.2 Ez 8:1–3

> **1** In the sixth year, in the sixth month, on the fifth day of the month, as I sat in my house, with the elders of Judah sitting before me, the hand of the Lord God fell upon me there. **2**Then I looked, and behold, a form that had the appearance of a man. Below what appeared to be his waist was fire, and above his waist was something like the appearance of brightness, like gleaming metal. **3** He put out the form of a hand and took me by a lock of my head, *and the Spirit lifted me up between earth and heaven and brought me in visions of God to Jerusalem.*

Several things are noteworthy about this introduction to the following vision report: First of all, it is not clear *who is lifting the prophet up*: V. 1 introduces the hand of Yahweh that came upon the prophet. In v. 2, Ezekiel describes a heavenly being, whose identity is discussed among scholars. Leslie C. Allen holds the view that this being is Yahweh himself, especially because Ez 8:2 reminds the reader of Yahweh's glory in Ez 1:27.[7] However, if we take a closer look, the order of description is reserved and the being in Ez 8:3 has no brightness around him (but see Ez 1:27b-28). Besides that, the splendor of the being in Ez 8:3 is much less than in 1:26-

[6] Allen, *Ezekiel 1–19* (WBC 28), 43.

[7] Ibid., 279–280.

27 and even more, Ez 1:28 explicitly states that Ezekiel is describing the "appearance of the likeness of the glory of the LORD", an expression which is absent in Ez 8:2. Altogether, it is better to hold that the man in 8:2 is a heavenly being, an angel close to Yahweh, but not Yahweh himself.[8] V. 3a continues by saying that the heavenly being "put out the form of a hand", whereas in v. 3b, the spirit lifts the prophet up.

Even though it is not clear in the end who lifted the prophet up (the hand of Yahweh, the hand of an angel, or the spirit), all three beings are close to one another. We see the prophet groping for words in his struggle to describe his experience.

Secondly, *the place where Ezekiel is brought to* needs further explanation. Interestingly, two of the most read Thai versions differ in v. 3a:

TSV 2011	และทรงนำข้าพเจ้ามาถึงกรุงเยรูซาเล็มด้วยนิมิตของพระเจ้า *lae song nam khaphchao ma tueng krung Yerusalem duay nimit khong phrachao*
TNCV	และในนิมิตของพระเจ้านั้น พระองค์ทรงพาข้าพเจ้ามายังเยรูซาเล็ม *lae nai nimit khong phrachao nan phraong song pha khaphchao ma yang Yerusalem*
ESV	and brought me in visions of God to Jerusalem

The difference that we are concerned with here is that in the TSV 2011 Ezekiel is brought to Jerusalem *by means* of a vision of God (<u>ด้วย</u>นิมิตของพระเจ้า *<u>duay</u> nimit khong phrachao*), whereas according to the TNCV Ezekiel is brought to Jerusalem *in* a vision of God (ในนิมิตของพระเจ้า *nai nimit khong phrachao*).

The Hebrew has יְרוּשָׁלַ֫מָה בְּמַרְאוֹת אֱלֹהִים (*yĕrûšālamâ bĕmar'ôt 'ĕlōhîm*) and the question is, how בְּ (*bĕ*) is to best be understood

[8] Zimmerli, *Ezekiel 1* (Hermeneia), 236.

here: Is it meant to denote an instrument or an agent[9] ("he brought me to Jerusalem *by* visions")? Or does *bĕ* rather indicate a place?[10] He brought me to Jerusalem *in* visions? In the present report, I argue for this second option and take *bĕmar'ôt 'ĕlōhîm* as an additional phrase that explains the previous word (Jerusalem) in more detail.

The expression "the hand of the Lord GOD" (Ez 8:1, see 1:3), the presence of an angelic being that is close to the glory of Yahweh (8:2 reminds the reader of 1:27-28), the expression "between earth and heaven" (v. 3) are connections to the first vision of the book. This suggests that Ezekiel in this instance is brought into the heavenly realm. Like in Ez 1:1-3 he is under the power of Yahweh, but this time he does not only gaze into an open heaven, he enters heaven. The Jerusalem that he sees is *Jerusalem in divine visions.* Ezekiel is not brought to the historical Jerusalem and has a vision there, but Jerusalem here is part of Ezekiel's vision: This gets further support from the fact that Ezekiel suppresses the proper names Jerusalem and Zion in Ez 8–11, but only speaks of Jerusalem as "the city" (Ez 9:1,4,5,7,9; 10:2; 11:2.6.23); in Ez 9:4 "Jerusalem" is understood as later addition by most of the commentators.[11] Ez 9:8 and 11:15 mean Jerusalem on earth rather than the heavenly Jerusalem.

The report in Ez 8 about Israel's sins defiling the temple leaves the impression of stylistic systematization, timelessness, and historical distance. R. M. Hals writes: "It should be borne in mind throughout that, despite their detail, these scenes are not actual, historical ob-

---

[9] Bruce K. Waltke and M. O'Connor, *An Introduction to Biblical Hebrew Syntax* (Winona Lake: Eisenbrauns, 1990), 197.

[10] Waltke / O'Connor, *An Introduction to Biblical Hebrew Syntax*, 196.

[11] Zimmerli, *Ezekiel 1* (Hermeneia), 224; G. A. Cooke, *A Critical and Exegetical Commentary on the Book of Ezekiel*, The International Critical Commentary (Edinburgh: T. & T. Clark, 1985), 109; Allen, *Ezekiel 1–19* (WBC 28), 122.

servations, but reports of a transcendent experience in which the boundaries of time (including sequence) as well as space are described as fully surpassed".[12] Altogether, by letting Ezekiel see this transcendent structure God informs him about the hopeless defilement of Israel, which serves as a basis for Ez 9–11. Besides Ez 8:1-3, this is not the only change of place of the prophet in the whole of Ez 8–11, the second vision report of the book.

4.1.4.3 Ez 8:5-18

In *Ez 8:5–18* Yahweh himself[13] brings Ezekiel to different places within the temple precinct to show him Israel's abominations (v. 7,14,16). It is not mentioned that Yahweh lifts Ezekiel up.

4.1.4.4 Ez 11:1

In *Ez 11:1* however, the spirit lifts Ezekiel up and brings him to the east gateway of the temple. What the prophet experiences there will be examined in detail below (p. 66ff.), together with the analysis of the content of the visions.

4.1.4.5 Ez 11:24

Ez 11:24 is one of the closing verses of the vision report in Ez 8–11. As in Ez 3:12-15, the spirit lifts the prophet up and brings him back to the exiles in Babylon. This makes Ez 11:24 a perfect counterpart to the introduction of the report in 8:1-3. There, Ezekiel entered the unseen realm and now he leaves it again. In both cases Yahweh initiates and accompanies both the entering, and the leaving, of the unseen world with his Spirit.

---

[12] Hals, *Ezekiel* (FOTL 19), 61.

[13] Block, *The Book of Ezekiel: Chapters 1–24* (NICOT), 284.

4.1.4.6 Ez 37:1

> 1 The hand of the LORD was upon me, *and he brought me out in the Spirit of the Lord* and set me down in the middle of the valley; it was full of bones.

In this verse, there are several hints that point out that in Ez 37:1-14 Ezekiel reports about a vision he has received. The first one is the "hand of the Lord", that comes upon the prophet, which connects Ez 37:1-14 to the vision reports in Ez 1:11:1–3:14 ("hand of the Lord" in 1:3 and 3:14); Ez 8:1–11:25 ("hand of the LORD" in 8:1) and Ez 40–48 ("hand of the LORD" in 40:1). Secondly, the Spirit of the LORD is also mentioned in other vision reports of the book (Ez 3:12,24; 8:3; 11:1,5,24). Thirdly, as in other visions, the prophet has an experience of translocation, as he is transported to another place (like in 8:3; 11:1,24; 40:1-2). If we take all those observations together, it is clear that Ez 37:1-14 is a vision report.

As in Ez 8:3 (see above p. 48f.) the prophet is brought to another place, in this case it is a valley (like in Ez 3:22-23). The valley is not mentioned, maybe because the vision itself is more important than the exact place. In addition to this, Daniel L. Block assumes that the valley was well known to Ezekiel and his audience as the Hebrew word for valley has the article (as in 3:22).[14] As the "he" in "he brought me" finally points out, it is the LORD who (by using his hand) brings Ezekiel to the valley.

4.1.4.7 Ez 40:1-2

> 1 In the twenty-fifth year of our exile, at the beginning of the year, on the tenth day of the month, in the fourteenth year after the city was struck down, on that very day, the hand of the LORD was upon me, and *he brought me to the*

---

[14] Daniel I. Block, *The Book of Ezekiel: Chapters 25–48*. New International Commentary of the Old Testament (Grand Rapids: Eerdmans, 1998), 373.

city. 2 In visions of God *he brought me* to the land of Israel, and set me down on a very high mountain, on which was a structure like a city to the south.

Once again, the hand of the LORD came upon Ezekiel and brings him to a different place. In this case, the Spirit does not seem to be involved as much as in other visionary experiences (Ez 3:12; 8:3; 11:1,24; 37:1).

Additionally, we also have to take note of where the prophet is brought to. Even though Ezekiel is being brought to different spots inside the temple (Ez 40:17,24,28,32,35,48; 41:1; 42:1.15; 43:1,5; 44:1,4; 46:19,21; 47:1,2,6), his journey starts in Ez 40:1: The destination of the prophet's journey in v. 1 is generally referred to as "to the city", then as "land of Israel" (v. 2a) and then as "very high mountain" (v. 2b). Although the prophet suppresses "Jerusalem" and "Zion" as names like in Ez 9–11 (see above p. 50), Ezekiel wants to say that he is brought to Zion/Jerusalem. This gets further support from Ps 48:2-3 and Is 14:13-14, where Zion is described as a very high mountain, because Yahweh dwells on it: "The 'very high mountain' represents theological geography and points to Yahweh's supremacy: cf. Is 2:2. Mount Zion is in view (cf. 17:22; 20:40)".[15] However, the city and the mountain mentioned here are *not* Jerusalem or Zion as earthly realities; they are rather part of the visionary experience of the prophet. The place where Ezekiel is brought to, inside the visionary reality, is the transcendent counterpart to earthly Zion. This concept will be discussed in detail below on p. 62ff.

After Ezekiel has been brought to Mount Zion in the heavenly realm, his journey seems to only begin there. As in Ez 8:5-18; 11:1, a man "whose appearance was like bronze" (40:3), obviously a heavenly being lesser than Yahweh, guides the prophet through the temple complex (40:17,24,28,32,35 and others), measures certain

---

[15] Allen, *Ezekiel 20–48* (WBC 29), 229.

structures (40:6-14,19-27; 41:1-5; 42:15-20 and others) and sometimes interprets what Ezekiel sees (42:13-14 and others).[16] We therefore find many instances where the prophet is brought or led to another place. In Ez 43:5 the spirit lifts Ezekiel up and brings him to the inner court, thereby highlighting the fact that Yahweh's Glory fills the temple – the place where God will dwell in the midst of Israel (v. 7).

4.1.5 Interim Summary

In the various opening and closing sections covered above, the prophet Ezekiel describes what happened to him both when he received visions from God, and when the visions left him; however, note that both vision 3 (Ez 37:1-14) and vision 4 (Ez 40–48) do not have any closing sections.

There are certain elements that occur in the introduction of every vision report and other elements that are unique but important.

Starting with the unique element: Only vision 1 (Ez 1–3) has the opening of the heavens which means that Ezekiel gets access to the transcendent and unseen realm, the world of God and the divine beings. Besides that, there are four elements that occur in every introduction of a visionary report.

1. Every vision report (except vision 3; Ez 37:1-14) gives the precise date when Ezekiel received the vision: God gave the visions 1 and 2 (Ez 1–3 and Ez 8–11) between the first and the second exile of the Judeans, between 592 and 587 B.C.; vision 4 (Ez 40–48) God gave after the destruction of Jerusalem (587 B.C.).
2. Another element that is found in every vision is that the hand of Yahweh comes over the prophet. As the hand represents power,

[16] Allen, *Ezekiel 20–48* (WBC 29), 229; Block, *The Book of Ezekiel: Chapters 25–48* (NICOT), 514.

this means that the prophet is fully under the power of God when he receives a vision.

3. Besides that, in every vision, Ezekiel is lifted up and brought to another place. Usually these movements are a result of the working of the spirit of Yahweh (Ez 3:12-14; 8:3; 11:1.24; 37:1). On the basis of the texts we cannot decide whether it is only the spirit of Ezekiel that travels somewhere else, while his body stays where it is, or whether it is both spirit and body that makes the trip. The Bible text, as it is, does not suggest dividing Ezekiel as a person. He seems to travel as a whole; not only parts of him. This will be further discussed in Chapter 5.

To sum up: When receiving a vision, the prophet Ezekiel was granted access to the unseen realm, the space where God dwells. It is unique though, that in that sphere, the prophet is able to walk in the temple and its buildings, to talk with Yahweh, and to see his divine throne and his glory. As he is a human being, he stands out among all the heavenly beings, and this might be the reason why he is called "son of man" throughout the book. Allen writes: "Ezekiel is a 'human being and no God […], out of his league in the transcendent scene".[17] As we will see in the next section in the report, Jerusalem and the temple are the heavenly counterparts of the earthly Jerusalem and the temple (for more details of this concept refer to p. 62f.).

4.2 The Content of the Visions

After the introductions and closing sections of the four vision reports in the Book of Ezekiel have been analyzed, I will, in this section, focus more on the content of the visions themselves. However, the exegesis that will be done here will not go into the details of

[17] Allen, *Ezekiel 1–19* (WBC 28), 38.

every vision report. The aim is rather to grasp the message as a whole of each vision report.

4.2.1 The Vision of the Throne of God (Ez 1–3:15)

Although there are different opinions about how this vision is to be divided into sections, the easiest approach seems to be according to what Ezekiel sees:[18]

- In 1:4 – 1:28 Ezekiel sees the Glory of the LORD; a speech from Yahweh (2:1 "*I heard the voice of someone speaking*") follows and comes to an end in Ez 2:7 with the words "*whether they hear or refuse to hear*".
- In 2:9-10 Ezekiel sees a "*scroll of a book*", followed by a speech from Yahweh until 3:11. This speech has the same closing as 2:7 ("*whether they hear or refuse to hear*").

Thus, the outline of the vision Ez 1:1-3:15 is as follows:

Introduction (Ez 1:1-3)

1:4-28	*vision*: Ezekiel *sees* the Glory of Yahweh
2:1-8	*audition*: Ezekiel *hears* Yahweh's first speech
2:9-10	*vision*: Ezekiel *sees* a scroll in Yahweh's hand
3:1-11	*audition*: Ezekiel *hears* Yahweh's second speech

Conclusion (Ez 3:12-15)

As the present study is about the visionary experiences of Ezekiel, the focus will be on Ez 1:1-28 and on 2:9-10 more so than on the other parts of this visionary section of the book.

---

[18] Behrens, *Prophetische Visionsschilderungen*, 185-186.

4.2.1.1 The Vision of the Glory of Yahweh (Ez 1:1–28)

Ez 1:1-28 is a long, detailed, and fascinating description of "the appearance of the likeness of the glory of the LORD" (Ez 1:28). According to the suggestion of A. Behrens, the vision consists of three parts, each one beginning with "and I saw" (*wāʾēreʾ*): Ez 1:4–14, 15–26 and 27–28.[19]

In the first part (v. 4–14) Ezekiel sees and describes four living creatures with four wings and four faces around burning coals of fire (v. 13). This portrayal of the four living beings makes use of individual images, which are documented in ancient Near Eastern iconography, accumulates them and condenses them into an impressive overall picture.[20] Taken all together, the four figures "reflect the universal power of God".[21] Greenberg quotes from a midrash to Exodus 15:1: "Four kinds of proud beings were created in the world: the proudest of all – man; of birds – the eagle; of domestic animals – the ox; of wild animals – the lion; and all of them are stationed beneath the chariot of the Holy One' … That is to say, the most lordly of creatures are merely the bearers of the Lord of lords".[22]

The next section (v. 15–26), begins with a description of four wheels (v. 15–21). The description mentions three times that the wheels are standing on the earth (v. 15.19.21). This fits well in regards to the material that the wheels are made of: Beryl; the Hebrew has *taršîš*. Following Greenberg, "the word might refer to bright yellow precious stone" or a "stone of dark red color, such as

[19] Behrens, *Prophetische Visionsschilderungen*, 185.

[20] Allen, *Ezekiel 1–19* (WBC 28), 27.

[21] Ibid., 28.

[22] Moshe Greenberg, *Ezekiel 1–20. A New Translation with Introduction and Commentary*, Anchor Bible 22 (Garden City: Doubleday, 1983), 56.

the carbuncle or ruby".[23] The yellow or red color of the stone might thus underline the fact that the wheels are standing in connection with the *earth.*

That there are four wheels, and that each wheel is full of eyes, together with their ability to move everywhere, shows the omnipresence and sovereignty of Yahweh *on earth*: Ez 1:17 (3x "went") and v. 19–21 (7x a form of "to go") expresses the idea of the portability of the wheels very clearly.

When Ezekiel described the four living creatures, he emphasized their agility as well (v. 9: 2x "went"; v. 12: 4x a form of "to go"). This complements omnipresence and domination of the *airspace* between heaven and earth.

In v. 22, the description moves on to the wings of the four living creatures that carry an expanse (v. 22, 23, 25, 26); the Hebrew has *rāqîa'*; the same word that is used in Gn 1 for the firmament that divides heaven from earth (Gn 1:6-8, 14-15, 17, 20; see Ps 19:2; 150:1; Dn 12:2). Above the firmament Ezekiel sees a throne and someone in human appearance sitting on the throne. In the given context, "throne" is clearly a symbol of kingship and power.[24] Since the bluish-shimmering plate is to be understood as the firmament,[25] the throne set up over the living beings and wheels means the comprehensive rule of the enthroned Yahweh over the entire airspace and over the whole earth from heaven.

His power extends completely over all three cosmic areas of air (the living beings in v. 4–14), earth (wheels in v. 15–25), and heaven (v. 26–28), the last two emphasizing the completeness of his rule in the sense of a merism as well as the four-number of living

---

[23] Greenberg, *Ezekiel 1–20* (AncB 22), 47.

[24] Joel F. Drinkard Jr., "Throne," in *The New Interpreters® Dictionary of the Bible 5*, ed. Katharine Doob Sakenfeld et al. (Nashville: Abingdon Press, 2009), 589.

[25] Allen, *Ezekiel 1–19* (WBC 28), 34.

beings, faces and wheels. The impression of sovereignty and full independence of Yahweh enthroned in heaven is not achieved through the description of his appearance, but through the description of his surroundings. Block stresses this point as one of the main theological issues of the vision:

> "The vision proclaims the sovereignty of Yahweh. All his attendants are noble creatures, but he is enthroned, the King over all! The universality of his reign is reflected in the prominence of the number four […], and especially in the absolute freedom with which heavenly chariot moves".[26]

That Yahweh reigns in full sovereignty is an important topic elsewhere in the book of Ezekiel. Ez 1:4–28 are thus connected with other passages in the book of Ezekiel, especially with those that announce the coming of Yahweh's kingdom in the future: Ez 20:33, 40-44 and Ez 43:5-7.

Other texts describe the future of Israel under the kingdom of God without mentioning it: According to Ezekiel, God's future kingdom includes a new exodus from all the countries of exile (see Ez 11:14-21; 20:33-38; 34:13-16; 36:24; 37:1-14), the renewal of the Israelites (see Ez 11:14-21; 36:25-27), a new covenant (see Ez 11:20; 34:25;36:28; 37:26-27) and the restoration of nature (see Ez 34:25-31; 36:8-11, 29-30, 34-35). The center of Yahweh's kingdom however, will be Mount Zion in Jerusalem (Ez 20:40-44; 34:26 and Ez 40–48 [especially 43:5-7]); the cult in the temple will play an important role in the kingdom of Yahweh according to Ezekiel.[27]

In Ez 1:4-28 however, Ezekiel receives a vision in which he sees Yahweh sitting on a throne, ruling as king over heaven and earth.

---

[26] Block, *The Book of Ezekiel: Chapters 1–24* (NICOT), 107.

[27] Florian Förg, "Present or Future Eschatology in Psalm 96 in the Light of Deutero-Isaiah," *Journal of Biblical Text Research* 36 (2015): 272; Florian Förg, "The Origins of Old Testament Apocalyptic Literature," in *Asia Journal of Theology* 31/2 (Oct. 2017): 71.

This kingly rule of Yahweh is exactly what the prophet announced for a time in the future elsewhere in his book. In Ezekiel's time, Yahweh was already reigning as king over heaven and earth; yet invisibly and only accessible in visionary experience. Only the future would bring the *visible revelation* of Yahweh's reign as king. In Ezekiel 1:4-28 Ezekiel becomes a witness that the kingly rule of Yahweh is already a reality in heaven. On earth, its revelation is still to come.

4.2.1.2 The Vision of the Scroll (Ez 2:9-10)

After Yahweh has called Ezekiel as a prophet (Ez 2:1-7), Yahweh lets him see a "hand stretched out" to him and "a scroll of a book" in it (v. 9). After the unnamed Yahweh has spread the scroll, it proves to be two-sided. Although scrolls with both front and back inscription are not unusual, in the given context this might mean that there is nothing more to add for the prophet: The message that Ezekiel receives is "not only a well-defined but also a complete message. Ezekiel may not modify it with his own comments, nor does God allow himself any room for adjustments".[28]

That the scroll contains "lamentation", "mourning", and "woe" (v. 10) does not so much point to the content of the scroll but rather to the effect of Ezekiel's message. As effects like these will only be triggered by prophecies of doom and judgment, those kinds of prophetic words were probably written on the scroll.[29]

Besides that, the vision of the scroll reminds the reader of Am 3:7 saying that "Yahweh reveals his secrets to his servants the prophets" and of Jer 1:9; in this verse, Yahweh stretches out his hand and puts his words in the mouth of Jeremiah. Ezekiel goes one step further: The words of God are now even written down in heaven and also known in their effects. The scroll-vision thus approaches the

---

[28] Block, *The Book of Ezekiel: Chapters 1–24* (NICOT), 124.

[29] Ibid., 125.

apocalyptic notion that future (and past) history is already known and established in the heavens above. D. S. Russel writes:

> "Not only did the apocalyptists divide up history into different periods of time; history, thus conceived, had been determined beforehand by the will of God and revealed to his servants. God had set down on the heavenly tablets the fixed order of events from which there could be no deviation whatsoever".[30]

In both Ez 1:4-28 and 2:9-10, Ezekiel gets access to the heavenly world, and what he sees there is connected to the future of Israel. Ezekiel sees the future of Israel that is already determined and fixed in the heavens.[31] Unlike Amos in his first two visionary experiences (Am 7:1-3 and v. 4-6), Ezekiel cannot change what God has planned to do. He can only fall to the ground (Ez 1:28) and swallow the scroll (Ez 3:2-3).

4.2.2 Ez 8-11: Ezekiel's First Temple-Vision

This visionary report divides into several parts: In transcendent reality, Yahweh shows the prophet several grievances in the temple in Jerusalem (Ez 8). This is followed by a report about six men that are going out to kill the inhabitants of Jerusalem (Ez 9). In the following chapters, Ezekiel sees the glory of the Lord leaving Jerusalem (Ez 10) and how Yahweh punishes the leaders of Israel (Ez 11:1-13). In the last section of the vision report, Ez 11:14-21, Yahweh promises to renew Israel (see above p. 59).

As we have seen previously (p. 50), Ezekiel has been given access by the hand and by the spirit of Yahweh (Ez 8:3) into this transcendent reality.

---

[30] David S. Russell, *Between the Testaments* (SCM Press: London, 1960), 106.

[31] Block, *The Book of Ezekiel: Chapters 1–24* (NICOT), 126-127.

As one reads the vision reported in Ez 8–11, it is crucially important to keep in mind that in Hebrew thinking the heavenly (or: transcendent) reality and the earthly (or: immanent) reality correspond to one another.

This means that the ancient Israelites believed that things here on earth have their counterparts in heaven: Besides the visible Jerusalem, a city in Israel, there also is a heavenly Jerusalem in the transcendent realm. This conception is also apparent in the Book of Revelation (ch. 21–22). Besides that, there is also a heavenly temple.

The writer of the Book of Hebrews makes use of this thought (Hebr. 8:5; 9:11, 23–24). Exodus 24:15-18 is clear on the fact that Moses has entered the cloud on Mt. Sinai, thereby entering the heavenly realm. There, Yahweh lets Moses see a model (Ex 25:9 ESV "pattern") of the tabernacle and its furniture. The sanctuary Israel will build has to follow the heavenly pattern exactly. To say it with the words of the writer of Hebrews: The temple in Jerusalem is only a copy of the true temple of Yahweh in heaven (Hebr. 9:24). "The tabernacle was intended to serve as a dwelling-place for God in the midst of his people on earth, and it would be completely in keeping current practice, that such an earthly dwelling-place should be a replica of God's heavenly dwelling place".[32]

4.2.2.1 Ez 8

In Ez 8, the prophet is taken to the heavenly, true temple of Yahweh. Greenberg writes: "What follows, is […] not to be taken as an account by an eye-witness in the flesh; *in a vision* Ezekiel 'went' to Jerusalem, and *in the same vision*, he 'returned' to Babylonia (11:24)".[33] Neither Ezekiel as a whole person nor only his soul

---

[32] Frederick F. Bruce, *The Book of Hebrews*, The New International Commentary on the New Testament (Grand Rapids and Cambridge: Eerdmans, 1990), 184.

[33] Greenberg, *Ezekiel 1–20* (AncB 22), 168.

alone are travelling to Jerusalem in Palestine, as one would not expect such blatant rites in the temple just thirty years after the reform of king Josiah (622 B.E.; 2 Kgs 22–23).[34] The Jerusalem Ezekiel finds himself in is the heavenly Jerusalem.

This is also the reason why Ezekiel seems to avoid the names "Jerusalem" or "Zion". He does not want his readers to miss the point by thinking he is staying in the earthly Jerusalem (see above p. 50). Besides that, Ez 8 does not have the Jerusalem of a certain time in mind. In the Jerusalem of the transcendent world, Yahweh[35] brings Ezekiel to different places in the heavenly temple in order to show him the totality of the cultic misconduct of Israel as a whole nation. This gets further support from the fact that the cultic sins of Israel are grouped in four pairs: We see men and women (v. 11.12.16 and v. 14), laity and priests (vv. 11.12. 16) worshipping Gods connected to the earth (Tammuz, v. 14-15) and the sun (v. 17), and deities both inside and outside the city (v. 5 and vv. 7-12.14.16-17). L.C. Allen confirms this view: Ezekiel sees a series of "religious sins that are rhetorically grouped together in the vision, but simply typical of worship on different times in Jerusalem at that period, which he himself may have seen while lived there".[36] Unlike ch. 9–11, the four scenes in ch. 8 do not constitute an anticipation of the future; ch. 8 is more likely to be written in order to provide reasons for the judgement announced in ch. 9–11.[37]

4.2.2.2 Ez 9

This chapter is closely linked to ch. 8, as it has the same place (the inner court of the temple), the same groups (the men before the house v. 6; mentioned in 8:16-18), and the same reason for pun-

---

[34] Block, *The Book of Ezekiel: Chapters 1–24* (NICOT), 299-300.

[35] Ibid.

[36] Allen, *Ezekiel 1–19* (WBC 28), 141.

[37] Hals, *Ezekiel* (FOTL 19), 52.

ishment (abominations, v. 4).[38] Besides that, A. Behrens points to the fact that the "seven men" of ch. 9 are not a part of the earthly, but of the heavenly reality.[39] Ez 9 thus continues the visionary report of Ez 8. If that should be true, there is no threshold between Ez 8 and Ez 9, and it therefore seems best to assume that the prophet still stays in the heavenly realm.[40]

The prophet hears Yahweh calling six men, each being armed with a weapon to destroy and to slaughter (Ez 9:1-2). These "supernatural destroyers"[41] remind the reader of the "destroyer" of the exodus tradition (Ex 12:23) and of the damage caused to Israel by angels (1 Sam 24:16-17; 1 Chr 21:14-17) or Assyrian troops (2 Kgs 19:35). Ezekiel develops this concept and sees six destroying angels, which, however, only appear as a group. In their individual descriptions they remain vague and thus all the more threatening. At the command of Yahweh, these destroying angels kill the inhabitants of Jerusalem both inside and outside the temple in the city (v. 7). Only the ones who sigh and groan over the abominations that Israel is committing against Yahweh will be spared (v. 4, 6). "Those who are marked for exemption are not merely the innocent or those who desist from evil, but those who are actively righteous – they moan and groan over the sins of the city", writes D. I. Block.[42]

That being said, it is striking that Ezekiel does not forget to add one small detail about the direction that the destroyers are coming from. Ez 9:2 says that they "come from the direction of the upper gate, which faces north." That the destroyers are coming from the north reminds the reader of the prophecies of Jeremiah, who insists on the fact that the Babylonians will come from the north to besiege

---

[38] Hals, *Ezekiel* (FOTL 19), 55-56.

[39] Behrens, *Prophetische Visionsschilderungen*, 226.

[40] Zimmerli, *Ezekiel 1* (Hermeneia), 246.

[41] Allen, *Ezekiel 1–19* (WBC 28), 146.

[42] Block, *The Book of Ezekiel: Chapters 1–24* (NICOT), 310.

and destroy Jerusalem (Jer 1:13-19; 4:6; 6:1,22; 10:22; 13:20; 25:9). There seems to be a deliberate connection between Jeremiah's enemy from the north and the destroyers in Ez 9.[43]

If this is true, then what Ezekiel sees in the heavenly realm anticipates the fact that many people in Jerusalem will be killed during the destruction of Jerusalem in 587 B.C. by Babylonian troops. As Ezekiel has received this vision in 592 B.C., there are roughly five years between the visionary anticipation and the realization of this event on earth. In his commentary W. Eichrodt writes: "No information, of course, is here supplied as to the historical details of the fall of Jerusalem. What we are given here, is the metaphysical background of it all".[44]

Moreover, the coming events seem already to be determined and somehow scheduled in the transcendent reality. This is clear from two facts: First, that Yahweh orders the destroyers to carry out the judgement (Ez 9:1,5-7), and secondly, even Ezekiel the prophet is unable to stop the judgement of Yahweh through his intercession (v. 8-10). His only hope is that Yahweh will spare some Israelites as a remnant (v. 4-11).

4.2.2.3 Ez 10

The prophet continues his visionary report. Once again, a "solely transcendent reality is made visible to the prophet's eye alone in order that he could […] understand the deeper meaning of the visible events of the city's destruction".[45]

Even more so than Ez 8–9, Ez 10 describes the environment of the throne of Yahweh and strongly reminds the reader of Ez 1. In Ez 10, however, the prophet depicts how Yahweh's glory leaves the

---

[43] Allen, *Ezekiel 1–19* (WBC 28), 146.

[44] Walther Eichrodt, *Ezekiel. A Commentary*, The Old Testament Library (London, SCM Press, 1970), 130.

[45] Hals, *Ezekiel* (FOTL 19), 72.

heavenly counterpart of the temple of Jerusalem from the Cherub (over the Ark of the Covenant to the threshold of the temple-building; Ez 10:4), then to the entrance of the east gate of the temple (v. 18-19). Finally, the glory of Yahweh leaves the city of Jerusalem (Ez 11:23). We should try to understand that, in this event, Ezekiel sees the heavenly reality in the light of Ez 9. Just as many Israelites will be killed when Nebuchadnezzar and his troops take Jerusalem (Ez 9), the glory of Yahweh will also leave the city (Ez 10), making the temple an empty building that the Babylonians will plunder and burn down. R. M. Hals points out that the desecration of the temple is not the result of an offensive, or hostile, action of outsiders: The Babylonians do *not* have the power to force Yahweh to leave his temple; Yahweh voluntarily withdraws from it.[46]

But there is another event that, according to Ez 10, will happen at the same time when Yahweh's glory will leave Jerusalem: The city will be destroyed by fire, an event that is anticipated in Ez 10:1-8. Yahweh calls the man clothed in linen (obviously the same man as in Ez 9:2-4, 11) to take burning coals from between the wheels that carry the throne of Yahweh and to scatter them over the city (Ez 10:2). Greenberg is right, when he writes on Ez 10:2 that "this vision meant the doom of the city had been sealed. Earthly events were merely the working out of this antecedent decree".[47] Once again, what Ezekiel sees in the transcendent reality, anticipates events yet to come true on earth. Unlike in Ez 9, Ezekiel raises no objections and appears as a mere spectator or bystander. No one can stop the coming of these events anticipated and fixed in the unseen realm of Yahweh.

4.2.2.4 Ez 11

This is the last chapter in this visionary report, and the events narrated in Ez 11 still take place in the visionary transcendent world.

---

[46] Hals, *Ezekiel* (FOTL 19), 72.

[47] Greenberg, *Ezekiel 1–20* (AncB 22), 181.

This is especially obvious from the fact that Ez 11 is connected to Ez 8 as follows:

Ez 11:1 ("the Spirit lifted me up and brought me to") resembles Ez 8:3, but also 8:7, 14 and 16. The fact that the scene in Ez 11:1-13 plays at a gate (Ez 11:1) creates a special connection to Ez 8 (v. 3, 5, 14), but also to Ez 9–10 (9:2; 10:19). In addition to that, the name *Ya'ăzanyâ* (son of *'Azzur*, Ez 11:1) reminds the reader of *Ya'ăzanyāhû* (son of *Šāpān*, Ez 8:11). If one considers the connecting lines between Ez 8 and Ez 11, it is possible to speak of an *inclusio* that holds together the first vision of the temple in the Book of Ezekiel: The social offenses of Ez 11 form a suitable complement to the cultic transgressions of Ez 8.

L.C. Allen is surely right when he calls Ez 11 "a further visionary temple scene".[48] As the scene is located in the transcendental reality, *Ya'ăzanyâ* the son of *'Azzur* and *Pělaṭyāhû* the son of *Běnāyāhû* (v. 1b) are transcendent beings that we should not understand historically. This gets further support from the fact that we lack any information about who those two persons have been historically.[49] According to D. I. Block, both names (*Ya'ăzanyâ* and *Pělaṭyāhû*) were quite popular in the end of the 6th century B.C.[50]

The names have rather been chosen because of their meaning: *Ya'ăzanyâ* means "Yahweh hears" or "Yahweh has heard" and *'Azzur* "one who has been helped"[51]. Thus, *Ya'ăzanyâ* the son of *'Azzur* points to the time after exile of 597 B.C. We know from the account in 2 Kings (24:16 and 25:11-12) that there were Judeans left behind in Jerusalem, who received Yahweh's help in the city.

---

[48] Allen, *Ezekiel 1–19* (WBC 28), 131.

[49] Zimmerli, *Ezekiel 1* (Hermeneia), 257.

[50] Block, *The Book of Ezekiel: Chapters 1–24* (NICOT), 331.

[51] Ludwig Koehler and Walter Baumgartner, *The Hebrew and Aramaic Lexicon of the Old Testament* 2, ed. M.E.J. Richardson (Leiden / New York / Köln: E.J Brill, 1995), 812.

Block gives further details on their roles: "Jaazaniah and Pelatiah were obviously political counselors of some sort. They undoubtedly represented the *nouveau noblesses* who filled the political vacuum left when Jehoiachin and the established nobility were deported to Babylon (2 Kgs 24:10-17)."[52]

However, as leaders of the people (v. 1), they started to acquire the property of those who had to leave Jerusalem as exiles (Ez 11:2-3). Their inner attitude is clearly expressed in the proverb "This city is the cauldron and we are the meat" (v. 3). In order to enforce their claims successfully, they use their power selfishly (v. 2) and they do not shy away from murder (v. 6-7). It looks like Ezekiel invents two persons that stand for the "leaders of the people" as a whole and gives them artificial names to characterize them: Yahweh has helped them (*'Azzur*), and he hears (*Ya'ăzanyâ*) what they say and plan (v. 2-3).

Besides that, the name of the father of the second man *Bĕnāyāhû* (from Hebrew *b-n-h*, "to build") could possibly be connected with hope for the future, as announced in Jer 1:10; 18:7-10; Ez 36:35-36. His death (v. 13) therefore warns the leaders of Israel, after the first exile, (597 B.C.) that they will not have any hope for the future: Yahweh will not "build" them (*Bĕnāyāhû*) and will not save them, as *Pĕlaṭyāhû* means (from Hebrew *p-l-ṭ*, "to save").[53] The name of the second of the two princes seeks to communicate that even though Yahweh has saved some leaders in the incidents of 597 B.C., because of their exploitation of the weak for their own enrichment, they will have no future. This is exactly what Ezekiel prophesies in v. 8-10.

---

[52] Koehler / Baumgartner, *Hebrew and Aramaic Lexicon*, 332. This is confirmed by *śārê hā'ām*, the last words of v. 1, which clearly characterize both *Ya'ăzanyâ* and *Pĕlaṭyāhû* as leaders.

[53] Block, *The Book of Ezekiel: Chapters 1–24* (NICOT), 331.

After all, how should we understand the sudden death of *Pĕlaṭyāhû* the son of *Bĕnāyāhû*? It seems best to understand it in the very same way as we have already understood Ez 9 and 10: His death is an anticipation of events that will happen on earth in the future. According to 2 Kgs 25:18-21, upper class citizens of Jerusalem were brought to Riblah at the border of Israel and were killed there by the King of Babylon in the course of the destruction of Jerusalem. In 587 B.C. the events Ezekiel had seen in the heavenly realm finally came true. "The destruction which has been announced takes place symbolically before the prophet's own eyes, upon one of the figures seen by him".[54]

After these visionary reports, the section Ez 8–11 draws to an end, Ez 11:14-21 and Ez 11:1-13 standing in sharp contrast, yet corresponding to one another. As Ez 11:1-13 addressed the remaining people in Jerusalem (v. 9), Ez 11:14-21 now addresses the Israelites already in exile among the nations. Unlike the princes remaining in Jerusalem who had no future, the Israelites in exile are promised that Yahweh will save them, bring them back, and give them a new heart (Ez 11:17-19). They thus will be faithful to Yahweh (v. 20), quite the opposite of the unfaithful leaders remaining in Jerusalem (v. 12).

4.2.3 Ez 37:1-14: The Valley of Dry Bones

As mentioned above, Ez 37:1-14 is also a vision report, mainly because several features in v. 1 connect this text with the previous (Ez 1–3 and 8–11) and following vision reports (Ez 40–48); those are "the hand of the LORD" (Ez 1:3; 3:14 [vision 1]; 8:1 [vision 2] and 40:1 [vision 4]), the activity of the spirit (Ez 3:12,24; 8:3; 11:1,5,24) and the dislocation of the prophet (Ez 8:3; 11:1,24; 40:1-2). Thus R. M. Hals is right when he states that, "The present pas-

---

[54] Zimmerli, *Ezekiel 1* (Hermeneia), 259.

sage is by far the briefest of the four visions, though certainly the most famous".[55]

The vision report divides into v. 1-10 and v. 11-14; W. Zimmerli has explained the relationship between the two parts as "image and interpretation, where the interpretation contains at the same time the real proclamation to the people".[56]

Unlike the other three visions in the book of Ezekiel, this vision is not given a date. This has led some scholars to the conclusion that the date has been lost by some textual accident, but this is only speculation. At least it is clear from the people's view of themselves in v. 11 that this passage is set in the exilic period, after the fall of Jerusalem in 587 B.C.[57]

In v. 1-10 Ezekiel finds himself in a valley full of dry bones and Yahweh tells him to prophecy first to the bones (v. 4-8) and then to the breath (v. 9-10). In the end, the dry bones have become a great army (v. 10). The symbolic action that Ezekiel is performing in the vision and thus in the transcendent realm, is explained in v. 11-14. The dry bones are a symbol for "the whole house of Israel" (v. 11), who are in Babylon, far away from the LORD, being punished by the LORD and therefore cut away from the source of life: "As in 33:10, the exiles after 587 B.C. view themselves as within the realm of death, existing only in '*resigned despair*'".[58]

In summary, the vision foreshadows a new exodus, a return to the country; it "expresses the event of the restoration and the regathering of the politically defeated all-Israel".[59] Thus this vision is not about a resurrection of the dead (even though it has been misunder-

---

[55] Hals, *Ezekiel* (FOTL 19), 269.

[56] Zimmerli, *Ezekiel 2* (Hermeneia), 257.

[57] Hals, *Ezekiel* (FOTL 19), 270.

[58] Ibid., 269.

[59] Zimmerli, *Ezekiel 2* (Hermeneia), 264.

stood as such many times), but about the *resurrection of Israel as a nation*. The return of the exiles is an event that Ezekiel expected for the future (see Ez 36:10; 39:25-27 and above p. 59), and besides that, the sequel to the present passage (Ez 37:15-28) will elaborate on the design of the resurrected nation.[60] Ez 37:1-14 is undoubtedly an anticipation of this future event in transcendent reality.

Additionally, it is apparent that this event is symbolically encrypted. In place of the exiles living in Babylon, a large amount of dead bones appears. Their resurrection stands for the return of the exiles to their homeland. Furthermore, D. I. Block points out that the dry bones represent the entire house of Israel (v. 11), including those Israelites who had been deported to Assyria after the fall of Samaria in 721 B.C. (2 Kgs 17).[61] The scope of the passage thus reaches further than just to the exiles in Babylon.

Besides that, there is one fact that makes this vision quite unique: Ezekiel is very much involved in the visionary events. Through his prophecy (v. 7.10) he seems to bring, or better speak, the events into existence; both the resurrection of the bones and the coming event of the new exodus. Even though Yahweh orders Ezekiel to prophecy and thereby takes the initiative, Ezekiel still has an important role in bringing about the future of Israel. Thus this vision is linked to Ez 8-11, where Ezekiel by prophesying brings about the death of *Pělaṭyāhû* the son of *Běnāyāhû* (Ez 11:13).[62]

4.2.4 Ez 40–48: Ezekiel's Second Temple-Vision

4.2.4.1 Outline

The whole of Ez 40–48 divides into three parts: After the introduction in Ez 40:1-4, the first part (Ez 40–46) is devoted to the descrip-

---

[60] Block, *The Book of Ezekiel: Chapters 25–48* (NICOT), 380.

[61] Ibid., 379.

[62] Zimmerli, *Ezekiel 1* (Hermeneia), 259-260.

tion of the temple, its buildings, gates, and furniture. One heavenly being takes Ezekiel on a temple tour and shows him all of this. The second part, Ez 47:1-13 ("Water Flowing from the Temple"), draws the attention of the reader away from the temple to the land. After that, Ez 47:13–48:35 describes the borders and the division of the land of Israel.

Ez 40:1-3, as an introduction to the visionary event in Ez 40-48, strongly recalls previous visions (Ez 1:1-3; 8:1-3; 37:1).[63] Therefore, one will have to assume that the prophet once again enters the reality invisible to the outside world. Ezekiel has an "experience of transcendent reality" and is "given access to the presence of Yhwh," writes Steven Tuell.[64]

4.2.4.2 Ezekiel's Temple Tour

After Ezekiel is brought to the transcendent realm, he encounters a man whose appearance is like bronze (v. 3a). He reminds the reader not only of the four living beings in Ez 1 (bronze in v. 7), but also to other male figures Ezekiel has met before in the transcendent world: the man in Ez 8:2 composed of fire and gleaming metal, the destroyer figures of Ez 9:1-2, and the man clothed in linen (Ez 9:2-3, 11; 10:2-3a, 6). Like those men, he also belongs to the transcendent, divine world. As his equipment, a linen cord and a measuring rod (v. 3) indicates, his task consists primarily in guiding Ezekiel through the heavenly temple buildings and in measuring the visionary temple. The movements of Ezekiel and his angelic "tour guide" are as follows – roughly spoken, the prophet moves from the outside to the inside, getting more and more close to the center. The route of Ezekiel in Ez 40-46 reminds the reader of Ez 8,

[63] Block, *The Book of Ezekiel: Chapters 25–48* (NICOT), 514.

[64] Steven S. Tuell, "Ezekiel 40–42 as Verbal Icon," *The Catholic Biblical Quarterly* 58 (1996): 649.

where Ezekiel and his guide took a similar journey from outside to the inside.[65]

4.2.4.3 Three Misunderstandings of the Temple Description

The description of the temple has been understood by scholars in different ways. The following are three of the more important, yet different, interpretations:

1. *A Blueprint of the First Temple*: In Ez 40–42 the multiple structures of the temple are measured in a two-dimensional outline; heights are almost never given (except for Ez 40:5). For this reason, many scholars have concluded that "Ezekiel's vision is based on a plan or blueprint of the first temple which he had either preserved himself or found in the archives.[66] Scholars like G. A. Cooke or W. Zimmerli have followed this idea.[67] Steven Tuell however argued against this by pointing out that "Ezekiel's vision does not conform to the pattern of the first temple".[68]
2. *A Building Proposal for the Second (Postexilic) Temple*: Other commentators have understood Ezekiel's temple description as a plan for the second temple that is meant for the Jews returning from exile to use in rebuilding the temple in Jerusalem. Among others, authors like John W. Wevers[69] and Moshe Greenberg[70] have supported this view, even though essential information for the construction (heights or building materials) is lacking. Ste-

---

[65] Block, *The Book of Ezekiel: Chapters 25–48* (NICOT), 515.

[66] Tuell, "Ezekiel 40–42 as Verbal Icon", 649-650.

[67] Cooke, *Ezekiel* (ICC), 425; Zimmerli, *Ezekiel 2* (Hermeneia), 412.

[68] Tuell, "Ezekiel 40–42 as Verbal Icon", 650-651.

[69] John W. Wevers, *Ezekiel* (London: Oliphants, 1969), 208.

[70] Greenberg, *Ezekiel 1–20* (AncB 22), 15.

ven Tuell holds the view that "we cannot even begin to construct Ezekiel's temple on the basis of these measurements".[71]

3. *An Eschatological Building Program*: Among others, Walther Eichrodt and Joseph Blenkinsopp have suggested that Ez 40–42 are meant as a description of the eschatological temple that Yahweh will build in the last days.[72] Against this view it can be said that Ezekiel is walking through an existing structure and his vision is not given a future setting.[73]

For the following reasons, the temple description is not meant as a blueprint of the first temple, nor a building proposal for the second temple. Concerning the third idea (the temple that Yahweh will build in the end times), the vision surely points to the future of Israel, when God reveals his kingdom on earth (see below p. 79ff.). Ezekiel however does not yet call this time the "end times".

I would consider the points Tuell has mentioned convincing. I would like to underline the fact that there is not one single verse in Ez 40–48 that requests Israel to build the new temple according to Ez 40–48: "Nowhere in this text do we find either a decision to build the temple, or a divine permission given for its building".[74] At this point, Ez 40–48 is standing in contrast to other temple building texts in the Old Testament, where Moses (Ex 25:8-9), David (2 Sam 7:4-7; 1 Chr 22:7-8; 28:1-4), or Solomon (2 Sam 7:13; 1 Kgs 5:17-19; 1 Chr 22;5-19 and others) are either commanded or denied permission to build the temple. Ez 43:10-11 only commands Israel to perform certain cultic activities in it.[75]

---

[71] Tuell, "Ezekiel 40–42 as Verbal Icon", 652.

[72] Ibid., 654.

[73] Ibid., 657.

[74] Tuell, "Ezekiel 40–42 as Verbal Icon", 652.

[75] Block, *The Book of Ezekiel: Chapters 25–48* (NICOT), 589; Allen, *Ezekiel 20–48* (WBC 29), 257.

Moreover, it is important to keep in mind that necessary information for building the temple, like height measurements and building materials, are missing. The only place where a certain height is measured is Ez 40:5: "So, he measured the thickness of the wall, one reed; and the height, one reed". Interestingly, there is a connection to the building instructions of the sanctuary in Ex 25–31: The mercy seat has to be constructed according to a specific length and width measurement, but there is no height specified: "Two cubits and a half shall be its length, and a cubit and a half shall be its breadth" (Ex 25:17). This observation could possibly be connected to the fact that both Ezekiel's envisioned temple and the mercy seat were understood as "the place of my throne and the place of the soles of my feet" (Ez 43:7; 1 Chr 28:2; Jer 3:16-17). As Yahweh dwells above the mercy seat / the temple, measuring the height is not only dangerous, but also obsolete.

More than that, the work of Th. Busink has shown that there are quite a lot of differences between Ezekiel's temple and Zerubbabel's temple which the Jews built after their return from exile. This concerns (among other things):

> the *front width* (Ez: 30 cubits / Zerubbabel temple: 60 cubits);[76]
>
> the *equipment of the vestibule* (Ez: with columns, Zerubbabel temple: no columns);[77]
>
> the *pedestal of the temple building* (Ez: 6 cubits ~ 3 meters / Zerubbabel temple: 1.5 meters);[78]

---

[76] Busink, Th. A. *Der Tempel von Jerusalem von Salomon bis Herodes. Eine archäologisch-historische Studie unter Berücksichtigung des westsemitischen Tempelbaus. 2. Band: Von Ezechiel bis Middot* (Leiden/Boston: Brill, 1980), 749, 812-813.

[77] Ibid., 818.

[78] Ibid., 819.

the *separation between Hekal and Debir* (Ez: flap doors / Zerubbabel temple: curtain);[79]

the *staircase to the altar* (Ez: stairs on the east side / Zerubbabel temple: ramp on the south side)[80]

and also the *outer courtyard* (the sanctuary of Jerusalem had no external courtyard around 300 B.C.,[81] even though Ezekiel describes the details in Ez 40:6-27).

This is further supported by Walther Zimmerli when he points out that when the exiles came back from Babylon, they did not distribute the land according to what we read in Ez 47:13–48:29:

> "Of this plan for the allocation of land, too, it must be stated that post exilic reality reveals no sign of its having been carried out. The complete disappearance of the former northern kingdom would certainly not lead us to expect anything else".[82]

To sum up, when rebuilding the temple, the Israelites did not follow Ez 40–48. Therefore, as we did not understand Ez 8–11 in a historical sense, we should not understand Ez 40–48 in the sense of a future temple that has to be built exactly according to the text.

4.2.4.4 The Twofold Purpose of Ez 40–48

1. *Israel Acknowledges its Sinfulness (Ez 43:10-11)*: This section gives further details of the purpose of the detailed description of the temple in Ez 40–46. Firstly, Ezekiel aims to make the Israelites feel "ashamed of their iniquities" (v. 10a) and he is doing so in describing "the design of the temple" (v. 11), "the exits and entrances" (v. 11) and the temple's "laws and the statutes"

[79] Busink, *Der Tempel von Jerusalem*, 819-820.

[80] Ibid., 828, 831.

[81] Ibid., 833.

[82] Zimmerli, *Ezekiel 2* (Hermeneia), 541.

(v. 11) – meaning the cultic activities that will be performed in it. “This spiritual map of holiness puts them [the Israelites, F.F.] in their place”, writes Daniel I. Block. “They are sinners visited by God, and invited to his presence by grace alone. Even in the new order, they do not earn the right to divine favor. Yahweh returns on his own initiative and for his own purposes”.[83] This points towards the fact that the description has a more spiritual purpose than it is a plan for building the second temple.

This might be combined with the view of Steven Tuell, who argues that Ez 40–48 describes “an actual visionary journey to the heavenly temple”[84] that stands atop of the heavenly Mount Zion.[85] As mentioned above (p. 75), height measurements are obsolete here, since Yahweh is coming to dwell in this temple. The text of Ez 40–48 is an attempt to mediate the presence of Yahweh in the heavenly sanctuary to the Israelites. “By means of Ezekiel’s report of his vision the exiles could share in this extraordinary experience, seeing in their mind’s eye the heavenly temple that Ezekiel saw”.[86]

One more hint towards this is the observation that both Ezekiel’s temple and the land show a symmetrical and harmonious regularity. In the architecture of the temple, the number 25 plays a central role: A total of 25 steps lead to the temple house, the gate buildings measure 25 x 50 cubits (Ez 40:21,25,28,32,35), the temple house 50 x 100 cubits,[87] the inner court 100 x 100 cubits (Blenkinsopp 1990, 205), the entire complex 500 x 500 cubits (Ez 42:20) and the area for the Levites, priests and the city 25,000 x 25,000 cubits (Ez 48:20).

---

[83] Block, *The Book of Ezekiel: Chapters 25–48* (NICOT), 589.

[84] Tuell, “Ezekiel 40–42 as Verbal Icon“, 657.

[85] Ibid., 659.

[86] Ibid., 664.

[87] Block, *The Book of Ezekiel: Chapters 25–48* (NICOT), 541.

> "Therefore, in stressing the number twenty-five and its multiples, Ezekiel is likely embedding holiness and sanctification symbolism in the heart of his utopia".[88]

Besides that, the whole construction is described as a square, which was considered in ancient times as the epitome of perfection. Tuell writes: "The detailed description serves to give us an overwhelming sense of the symmetry and order in the temple's design".[89] Additionally, the uniform distribution of the country (Ez 47:14: "And you shall divide *equally* what I swore to give to your fathers."), as well as listings (Ez 47:15-20; 48:2-8 and 48:23-28), emphasize that this new temple is perfect in its order.

The equal distribution of land (Ez 47:14) transmits the idea that in the age to come there will be no accumulation of property in the hands of the rich. This started to become a serious problem in Israel in the 8th century B.C. Rainer Kessler describes the loan and credit system practiced by the Israelites as one of the major reasons for this development:

> "If the loan could not be returned, individual members of the family were sold into slavery, and then their possessions and property"[90] (own translation).
>
> "Due to over-indebtedness, a part of the Israelite farmers, who until then had been free on their own land, fall into a state of lack of property. They face those who, because of their property, are in a position to continue to lend money,

---

[88] Stephen L. Cook, *Ezekiel 38-48: A New Translation with Introduction and Commentary* (New Haven: Yale University Press, 2018), 165.

[89] Tuell, "Ezekiel 40–42 as Verbal Icon", 652.

[90] Rainer Kessler, *Sozialgeschichte des alten Israel. Eine Einführung* (Darmstadt: Wissenschaftliche Buchgesellschaft, 2006), 119.

> ultimately attracting more and more people into their dependency […] "[91] (own translation).

Various prophetic texts address this problem in the northern, as well as in the southern parts of the divided monarchy (Is 5:8-10; Am 2:6-11; 8:4-6; Mi 2:1-2).

The renewed land represents a creation that Yahweh has renewed and restored under his kingly rule. Ez 47:1-12 seeks to transfer the same message: The waters of the stream that renew of creation (v. 7-12) flow from the temple as the place where Yahweh is dwelling as king among the Israelites.

When Ezekiel describes the perfect order of the temple and of creation in detail (Ez 43:10-11), his listeners will surely feel ashamed. Because of their iniquities, they do not fit in this renewed creation Ezekiel is proclaiming.

2. *The Kingdom of Yahweh in a Renewed Creation (Ez 43:1-9)*: In order to get more comprehensive meaning of the whole of Ez 40–48, I will now take a closer look at Ez 43:1-9.

   This text takes a prominent position in Ez 40–48, as it is right in the center of Ez 40–46, which makes up the first section of Ez 40–48 (see above p. 71). Besides that, another observation highlights Ez 43:1-9: Right at the beginning of Ezekiel's temple tour, Ezekiel *enters* the temple area through the *outer east gate* (Ez 40:6-16) and it is exactly this gate, where he *leaves* the temple area in Ez 42:15 ("he led me out by the gate that faces east"). In Ez 42:15-17 the angel measures the temple area from outside.

   Now, in Ez 43:1, the angel brings the prophet to the *outer east gate for the third time* and the reader might wonder what is so important about the outer east gate? It is the glory of Yahweh,

[91] Kessler, *Sozialgeschichte des alten Israel*, 121.

and the prophet sees how it enters the temple building (Ez 43:2-5).

Ez 43:1-9 are meant to be read in the light of Ez 8–11 (Ezekiel's first vision about the temple) and of Ez 1–3 (Ezekiel's vision of the glory of Yahweh):

Ez 43:3 And the vision I saw was just like the *vision that I had seen when he came to destroy* the city,	Ez 8–11[92] ("destroy": 9:1)
and just like the *vision that I had seen by the Chebar canal.* And I fell on my face.	Ez 1–3 ("Chebar": 1:1,3)

In the next section, these connections and their implications on an understanding of the whole of Ez 40–48 will be examined. Yahweh's glory arrives from the east (43:2), moves through the outer and inner east gates and fills the temple house (43:4), thereby exactly contrasting the departure of Yahweh's glory from the temple and the city as recorded in Ez 10:4.18-19 and 11:23 (see above, p. 65ff.). Just as the departure of Yahweh's glory out of the heavenly temple anticipated the defilement of the temple and Yahweh's departure from his sanctuary in the context of the events of the fall of Jerusalem (587 B.C.), so Ez 43:1-5 anticipate Yahweh's return to his temple. Allen is surely correct when he writes: "The outer east gate, where the tour had begun in 40:6 and to which Ezekiel had been brought back in 42:15 […] is the closest point of entry for Yahweh's return to take up residence in the new, east-facing temple – just as it had been the way he had earlier left the old temple".[93] What Ezekiel sees in a vision with his own eyes, he had already prophesied in

[92] Hals, *Ezekiel* (FOTL 19), 302-303.

[93] Allen, *Ezekiel 20–48* (WBC 29), 256.

37:26-28. In his sanctuary, Yahweh will dwell among the Israelites forevermore.

Besides that, we have to read Ez 43:1-9 in light of Ez 1–3, especially in light of Ez 1:4-28; the vision of the glory of Yahweh. As we have seen above (p. 59), that vision anticipated that Yahweh will once again rule as a king over all three cosmic areas of air, earth and heaven. Ez 43:1-9 also express this idea:

First of all, the throne of Yahweh and his footstool (v. 7a) clearly indicate Yahweh's reign as king.[94] The entry of the glory of Yahweh into the temple house signifies the dawn of Yahweh's reign. However, Ezekiel avoids using the ordinary word for king (מֶלֶךְ, *melek*) as he understands Yahweh's kingly rule not politically, but primarily as a reign inside the temple-cult.

Secondly, we have to keep in mind that the temple in Ancient Near Eastern thought had a symbolical meaning. The temple was not only a building made of stone; it was also a model that symbolized the cosmos as a whole.[95]

Ez 40–42 clearly reflects the idea of the temple as a symbol for the cosmos. Even the carvings of palm trees in the gates (Ez 40:16, 22, 26, 31, 34, 37), on the walls of the temple building (Ez 41:18-20), and on the doors to the Holy of Holies (Ez 41:25) show that Ezekiel's temple was understood as a representative of creation. The cherubs that Ezekiel mentions, together with the palm ornaments (Ez 41:17-20), are there to pro-

[94] Drinkard, "Throne", 589.

[95] M. Ottoson, "הֵיכָל hêkhāl," in *Theological Dictionary of the Old Testament* 3, ed. Johannes G. Botterweck and Helmer Ringgren (Grand Rapids: William B. Eerdmans, 1978), 387.

tect nature.[96] Solomon's temple had already been decorated with those beautiful carvings (1 Kgs 6:29-36).

What strikes the reader though is the fact that Ezekiel's temple does *not have* a "sea" anymore, which had been a bronze basin (roughly 5 m diameter) in Solomon's temple and symbolized that Yahweh had tamed the chaos waters of the primeval sea in the beginning of creation. Does this imply that Ezekiel envisions a creation without any chaos, a world that is perfectly in order? If we keep in mind that the prophet had already announced the renewal of creation under the kingly rule of Yahweh elsewhere in his book (Ez 34:25-31; 36:8-11, 29-30, 34-35; see above, p. 59), this thought becomes plausible. The detailed symmetry and order of the temple might also point to a creation that has been renewed by God and is therefore perfectly in order again; there is no chaos, no sea anymore.

To sum up, Ez 40–48 anticipates, in a vision, that Yahweh will come back to Zion and will there establish his kingly rule over Israel and the whole creation. The schematized temple description in Ez 40–48 anticipates the renewal of creation. Both the kingly rule of Yahweh, as well as the renewal of nation has been announced by the prophet elsewhere in his book. In Ez 40–48, he already sees, as a present fact, what Yahweh will do in the future. Concerning the fulfillment of these visions, we cannot say when Yahweh's glory entered the new temple building that the Jews dedicated in 516 B.C. However, in the Enthronement Psalms (Ps 47; 93; 96–99) they celebrated that Yahweh rules as king over Israel, all the nations, and over all creation.[97] Inside the temple, Yahweh has just begun to reign as king and to restore creation.

---

[96] Block, *The Book of Ezekiel: Chapters 25–48* (NICOT), 558; Zimmerli, *Ezekiel 2* (Hermeneia), 1050.

[97] Förg, "Present or Future Eschatology", 275-279.

4.2.5 Interim Summary on the Content of the Visions

This summary will review and highlight important points in order to achieve the third objective of the present study: "What happened when Ezekiel received a vision?" (see above p. 14).

1. In Ez 1:4-28, the first part of vision 1 (Ez 1–3), Ezekiel sees in a vision that Yahweh is sitting on his throne, reigning as king over heaven and earth. As this is exactly what Ezekiel has prophesied elsewhere in his book, we can thus state that Ez 1:4-28 are meant to be a kind of announcement of the future. What Ezekiel sees in heaven anticipates the revelation of the kingdom of Yahweh on earth. The vision of the book scroll (Ez 2:8-10) makes use of the same theology. The events of the future are already established in the heavens above.
2. Vision 2 (Ez 8–11) is to be read as a set of four chapters: In Ez 8, Ezekiel is brought to the heavenly temple of Yahweh. Here the idea comes into play that both Jerusalem, and the temple, have a counterpart in the unseen realm. In that temple, Ezekiel sees the sins that Israel has been committing and is still committing. This serves as a basis for Ez 9, which foreshadows in 592 B.C. that roughly five years later (587 B.C.) many Jerusalemites will be killed when Nebuchadnezzar takes Jerusalem. In that time, Jerusalem will be burnt down (Ez 10:1-8) and the glory of Yahweh will leave the city (Ez 10:4,18-19; 11:22-23). In Ez 11, the sudden death of *Pĕlaṭyāhû* the son of *Bĕnāyāhû* anticipates the time when leading upper class citizens were killed by Nebuchadnezzar in Riblah in 587 B.C. It is remarkable, though, how the heavenly realm is being reconstructed as a stage where the future events are displayed. Ezekiel has no chance of interacting with the players, he merely watches the events.
3. Ez 37:1-14 (vision 3) anticipates a new exodus of the Israelites out of Babylon into their homeland Israel and their resurrection as a nation. This exodus has already happened in the heavenly

realm and will happen on earth in Ezekiel's future. Indeed, after 539 B.C. after Cyrus's edict, many Israelites came back to Palestine from Babylon.

4. Ezekiel 40–48 (vision 4) anticipates in a vision that Yahweh will come back to Zion and will rule as a king over the whole creation. Ezekiel has announced this elsewhere in his book; this detailed vision report foreshadows it and lets the reader know that in heaven Yahweh has already accessed his throne (Ez 43:7-10) to rule as king. As can be seen from the Enthronement Psalms (Ps 47; 93; 96–99), the Jews believed that in the second temple (dedicated in 516 B.C.) Yahweh is reigning as a king.

So, what does it mean when an Old Testament prophet (Ezekiel) receives a vision? It means that Yahweh grants him access to the heavenly world. There he witnesses how the future events are made. Once they are established in heaven, they will surely come true on earth as well. It was the German scholar Klaus Koch[98] who introduced the term "Metahistorie" (metahistory) into the scholarly debate: Ezekiel sees processes that happen "meta" (behind or in the background of) the earthly history.

[98] Klaus Koch, "Das Reich der Heiligen und des Menschensohnes," in *Die Reiche der Welt und der kommende Menschensohn. Studien zum Danielbuch. Gesammelte Aufsätze Band 2*, ed. Martin Rösel (Neukichen-Vluyn: Neukirchener Verlag, 1995), 172.

5 Ezekiel's Visions in a Thai Context

5.1 Preliminary Considerations

The following section of the study will attempt to achieve the fourth objective described above (p. 14). The emphasis here will be on the ideas and concepts that Thai people have in mind when they hear, talk, or think about visions (rather than on discussing appropriate didactic approaches, teaching methods, or goals). All the points that will be mentioned in the following section are taken from personal interaction with students in a classroom setting and from literature.

Generally speaking, there is a huge interest in the Book of Ezekiel among Thai Christians. Part of this comes from the openness of Thai culture towards the unseen realm. Hoskin writes:

> "The vast majority of Thais, of course, are Buddhists. More than nine tenths of the population not only profess but also practice their faith. Yet the national religion overlays rather than supplants much older believes in unseen forces inhabiting a potent spirit world. (…) Manifest in beliefs concerning spirits and ghosts, as well as those regarding magical tattoos, charms, amulets, incantations, auspicious occasions, fortune telling, exorcism and other shamanistic rituals, the Thai involvement with the supernatural has its roots in ancient practices."[1]

Thai Christians then tend to connect their beliefs, experiences, and stories to what they read in the Bible. As a result of this, they have an enhanced interest in the visionary experiences of the prophet Ezekiel, the heavenly beings and structures he sees and especially in the process of receiving a vision. Their enhanced consciousness

---

[1] John Hoskin and Jean Leo Dugast, *The Supernatural in Thai Life* (Bangkok: Tamarind Press, 1993), 5.

for the supernatural world can be an important resource for understanding not only the Book of Ezekiel, but also other books and sections in the Old and New Testaments that contain vision reports. However, the Thai understanding of visions might differ from what has been discovered and studied in the Book of Ezekiel. It is thus the aim of this section to describe some common beliefs and concepts, that, for Thais, are connected to visionary experiences.

5.2 Ideas Concerning the Process of Receiving a Vision

5.2.1 Inducing a Vision

Thai people might possibly think that whenever someone receives a vision, one has to use certain means to induce the vision or prepare for it. Thai listeners might have heard about people using certain means in order to enter into different states of consciousness. In her book "Trance and Healing in Southeast Asia", Ruth-Inge Heinze writes that "Thai and Malay shamans enter trance seemingly effortless. After a brief period of meditation or some chanted evocations, they move into alternate states of consciousness".[2] Chinese mediums use

> "loud rhythmically reiterated sounds, drums, conch shell trumpets, clanging of bells, clashing and rattling of iron-ringed croziers, loud chanting of familiar words of power, dancing, inhaling of incense, and sudden shocks through noises and gestures" to induce trances.[3]

In the book of Ezekiel this seems not to be the case. When Ezekiel receives a vision, it finds him totally unprepared; this is reflected in the use of the verb "to fall" (נפל *n-p-l*) in connection to the hand of

---

[2] Ruth-Inge Heinze, *Trance and Healing in Southeast Asia Today* (Bangkok: White Lotus, 1988), 87.

[3] Ibid., 87, 90.

God. In Ez 8:1 the hand of Yahweh *falls* upon Ezekiel and in 11:5 the Spirit of Yahweh *falls* on the prophet. Like a shaman is possessed by an invoked deity, the prophet comes under the power of Yahweh, however, he did not prepare for it. It is only in the book of Daniel that a prophet prepared himself to receive visions by prayer and fasting (Dn 9:3).[4]

5.2.2 Possession by the Spirit or Deity

There are many stories circulating about experiences where a certain spirit entered into a person and inspires him to see visions or do extraordinary things.[5] Heinze relates how she once had encountered a Meo Shamaness in her village on Doi Suthep:

> "She 'rode' on a board into the spirit world. [...] Her chant reflected her ride through the spirit world. Once in a while she curbed her imaginary horse and called the spirit she just met. Naming him, she incorporated his power into her body. Such chanting may go on for one up to two full days, depending on the seriousness of the patient's illness. After several hours of 'riding' and charging her body with more spirit power, she felt prepared to cure a child who was suffering from a severe cold".[6]

Heinze has also observed and described spirit dances in Chiang Mai; where mediums, possessed by various spirits, meet and dance in order to entertain themselves and the spirits. Fermented green tea and hard liquor are involved as stimulants.[7]

---

[4] Martin Hengel, *Judentum und Hellenismus. Studien zu ihrer Begegnung unter besonderer Berücksichtigung Palästinas bis zur Mitte des 2. Jh. v. Chr.* Wissenschaftliche Untersuchungen zum Neuen Testament 10 (Tübingen: J.C.B. Mohr, 1969), 376.

[5] Heinze, *Trance and Healing,* 299.

[6] Ibid., 299.

[7] Ibid., 282-288.

For the book of Ezekiel, however, this is partly true, as it is clearly the Spirit of the Lord that transports the prophet to a certain place within the unseen realm (Ez 3:12-14; 8:3; 11:1.24; 37:1). It does not look like the Spirit is entering him, but Ezekiel surely gets under the power of Yahweh and his Spirit.

5.2.3 Losing Consciousness

Many Thai people, Christians as well as Buddhists, might believe that Ezekiel lost his consciousness when he received a vision. The texts that have been analyzed in the present study point the other way. Ezekiel's mind seems to be absolutely clear when he dwells in the transcendent realm. It is only his language that is limiting his ability to describe the heavenly things and beings he has seen with great detail.

5.2.4 Separation of Ezekiel's Soul from his Body

Whenever teaching about the visions of Ezekiel, students have asked if it is possible that only Ezekiel's mind or his spirit travelled somewhere else: Ezekiel's body has stayed in Babylon at the Chebar canal (Ez 1:1-3) while his mind or his spirit went to Jerusalem. This concept of a separation of an invisible part of the person (called soul, mind, or spirit) from the visible part (body) seems to be widely known.

A colleague, a missionary to Thailand, related that he once talked to a medium that had experienced a journey in a trance. She served *Mae Guan Im* (พระโพธิสัตว์กวนอิม) and was asked to cure a patient who was troubled by spirits and could not use his arm properly anymore. After she had been told the town and house number of the patient, the medium went into a trance to the hometown of the man and into his rubber tree plantation. The place was many kilometers away. There, she discovered something like four teeth growing out of one of the rubber trees. The medium then asked the patient about these "teeth". The man could remember that he had removed them and became ill afterwards. An offering to the spirit on this tree (half a chicken, incense, and half a bottle of liquor) helped him to use his arm normally.[8]

In this example it seems like the mind, or spirit, of the medium became detached from the body in order to travel somewhere else. The text of the book of Ezekiel however does not give any hint that this ever happened. This is because the Hebrews always saw a person as a whole, not composed of different parts that can easily disintegrate. Wallace puts it like this: “spirit […], soul […], body […], flesh […] are used according to the different aspects of man’s activity or being which it is intended to emphasize, but they must not be regarded as describing separate or separable parts which go to make up what man is”.[9] The words of Paul in his letter to the church in Corinth might help to understand this:

> *2 Cor 12:2* I know a man in Christ who fourteen years ago was caught up to the third heaven—whether in the body or out of the body I do not know, God knows. [3] And I know that this man was caught up into paradise—whether in the body or out of the body I do not know, God knows— [4] and he heard things that cannot be told, which man may not utter.

These four points above do not necessarily have to be taught; but they will help the teaching person to be prepared for the questions or contributions that the listeners might possibly have.

---

[8] Ernst Horn, *Von Schlangen, Geistern und liebenswerten Menschen: Heiteres und Nachdenkliches aus Thailand, dem Land der Freien* (Phayao: eg-Verlag, 2017), 107-108.

[9] R.S. Wallace, “Man,” In *The Illustrated Bible Dictionary 2*, ed. J. D. Douglas (Sydney / Auckland: Hodder & Stoughton, 1980), 941.

5.3 Ideas Concerning the Meaning of the Term *nimit* (นิมิต)

It is necessary to gain a basic understanding about the word *nimit*, as this is the preliminary understanding the listeners might possibly carry with them whenever they hear the word *nimit*.

First of all, following the *Thai Dictionary of the Royal Institute* of 2011 (พจนานุกรม ฉบับราชบัณฑิตยสถาน พ.ศ. ๒๕๕๔),[10] the term *nimit* is not a genuine Thai word, but is a Pali/Sanskrit term, that has been taken over into Thai language.[11] It can either be a verb or a noun.

The verb, which is of minor importance in the present report, means นิรมิต (*niramit*), สร้าง (*sang*), แปลง (*plaeng*), ทำ (*tham*):[12] "to construct, to create, to build, to manufacture, to form".[13]

The noun *nimit* can refer to the *sexual organs*[14] (อวัยวะสืบพันธ์ *awayawa sueb phan*), denotes a เครื่องหมาย (*a symbol*)[15] or refers to a good or bad omen ลาง (*lang*).[16]

---

[10] *Royal Institute Dictionary, BE 2554 (2011)*, Commemorating His Majesty the King's 7th Cycle Birthday Anniversary, December 5, 2011 (Bangkok, Siriwathana Inter Print, 2011) [in Thai].

[11] Ibid., 635-636.

[12] Ibid., 635.

[13] Wit Thiengburanathum, *Thai-English Dictionary (Library Edition)* (Bangkok: Ruamsan 1977), 490.

[14] *Royal Institute Dictionary*, 636; Thiengburanathum, *Thai-English Dictionary*, 490.

[15] *Royal Institute Dictionary*, 635; Thiengburanathum, *Thai-English Dictionary*, 207.

[16] *Royal Institute Dictionary*, 635, 1051; Thiengburanathum, *Thai-English Dictionary*, 815.

Besides that, *nimit* can have the same meaning as เหตุ (*hed*,[17] which denotes the *reason, cause* or *origin of something*[18]) or เค้ามูล (*khaumun*), which means *primary cause, motive, source* or *origin.*[19]

In a lecture about the visions in the Book of Ezekiel, one student noted that *nimit* always has *positive* connotations and refers to a positive omen, a positive foreshadowing, a sign for something positive that will happen in the future. Additionally, the student said that the word used in Thai for a negative omen is ลาง (*lang*).

According to the Dictionary of the Royal Institute, both *lang* and *nimit* can announce both positive and negative things in the future. Even the Dictionary of the Royal Institute has two examples:

> ผึ้งทำรังทางทิศตะวันออกของอาคารเชื่อกันว่าเป็นลางดี แมงมุมตีอกเชื่อกันว่าเป็นลางร้าย[20]
>
> *Phueng sang rang thang thid tawan og khong akhan chuea kan wa pen lang di maeng mum ti og chuea kan wa pen lang rai*
>
> Bees building a nest at the east side of the building are believed to be a good omen. Spiders beating their chest (against the wall and making a snapping sound) are believed to be a bad omen (own translation).

It appears as if *lang* is the genuine Thai word and *nimit* the Pali-Sanskrit word for both positive and negative omens or portends.

If compared with the content of the visions in the book of Ezekiel, *nimit* catches one central aspect of the visions of the book Ezekiel; they almost all (except for Ez 8) refer to the future (see p. 83f.) and are anticipating future events in Israel's history. All of these events

[17] *Royal Institute Dictionary*, 635.

[18] Thiengburanathum, *Thai-English Dictionary*, 1032.

[19] Ibid., 208.

[20] *Royal Institute Dictionary*, 1051.

have been announced elsewhere in the book, as well. The visions of Ezekiel thus should be understood as a special kind of prophesying the future.

The term *nimit* fits well because it is open to both negative and positive announcements: Whereas Ez 1–3 (vision 1), Ez 37:1-14 (vision 3), and Ez 40–48 (vision 4) prefigure Yahweh's reign as king (vision 1 and 4) and the resurrection of Israel as a nation (vision 3), Ez 8–11 are an announcement of judgement. In this vision Ezekiel has seen with his own eyes how Yahweh will judge Jerusalem (Ez 9:5-11) and how his glory will leave the temple (Ez 10:4.18-19; 11:23). Even though this is a negative, dangerous, and even destructive event, it still is called *nimit.*

As can clearly be seen from the Dictionary of the Royal Thai Institute, *nimit* also means "reason, cause" in some instances. This fits well to the visions of Ezekiel, as what Ezekiel sees brings the future into being in a sense. There is no space to intervene, not even for the prophet.

The one who will teach this set of lessons, however, should be aware of the following three points: Whenever listeners hear *nimit*, they might possibly think of something like the bees nest or spiders mentioned above that brings good or bad luck. The *nimit* Ezekiel has seen are not part of everyday experience; they are received in the unseen, heavenly realm. Secondly, it is the future of Israel as a nation that is at stake; not only the well-being of an individual or a family. Thirdly, there might be different opinions or even confusion among the listeners about what a *nimit* is, what a *lang* is and what they mean.

Yet there is another pre understanding of *nimit* that might occur in groups with a Christian background. They sometimes use the word *nimit* when they describe the "vision" of their church or organization. This use of vision/*nimit* might be called the "organizational use" and here *nimit* comes close to "goal", "aim", or "dream".

In almost every case, the envisioned goal or aim of the organization turns out to be something positive and good; so far the organizational use of the word fits well to the future aspect of *nimit*. On the other hand, receiving a *nimit* in the biblical sense means much more than “dreaming big” and aiming at a goal in the discomfort zone. One easily gets the impression that some organizations misuse the term *nimit* in order to highlight their own plans. Directly inspired from God, they cannot easily be criticized.

One final caveat: Whenever someone teaches Thai Christians about the visions of Ezekiel, he or she has to make sure that the listeners understand the historical background of the Book of Ezekiel. After having studied both Ezekiel, his times (p. 17ff.), the content, and the meaning of the visions, it should be clear that the visions cannot be separated from the events in history. God takes the events in Israel and Jerusalem serious; he speaks about them to his prophet Ezekiel and, through him, to all Israel. God’s message comes through Ezekiel to Israel *at a certain time and in a certain situation.* Although it has to be asserted that the Bible has meaning today, the message of the Bible has never come upon us without going to the first readers, or hearers, first. Hence, a thorough study of the historical circumstances of the Book of Ezekiel is indispensable. Whoever teaches or preaches about the visions of the book should under all circumstances include a sound introduction into the historical background of the Book Ezekiel.

6 Conclusion

6.1 Summary of Research Results

It has been the first objective of the present study to investigate the meaning of the terms חָזוֹן (*ḥāzôn*), מַרְאֶה (*mar'ê*), and מַחֲזֶה (*maḥăzê*). Research has shown that *ḥāzôn* and *maḥăzê* are both derived from the Hebrew root חזה (*ḥ-z-h*) as well as the verb *ḥāzâ*. Originally an Aramaic loanword, *ḥ-z-h* was used frequently in prophetic contexts to denote that a prophet received a word, a message from God. Although the general meaning of *ḥ-z-h* is "to see", no seeing is involved when the prophet receives the words of God.

The terms מַרְאֶה (*mar'ê*) and מַרְאָה (*mar'â*) however are derived from the root ראה (*r-'-h*) which is the genuine Hebrew term for "to see". Terms built from this root oftentimes appear in visionary contexts and denote the fact that the prophet literally sees divine beings and places in the heavenly realm.

Therefore, there seems to be quite a clear distinction between messages from God that the prophet *sees* (*r-'-h*) and messages that he *hears* (*ḥ-z-h*). On the other hand, it cannot be denied that prophetic visions include spoken words of God as well. This means that it is quite natural that in visions Yahweh speaks as well, Ez 1–3 being a good example for this (see above p. 56f.). Furthermore, one also has to keep in mind that in later times, this distinction seems to be softened up, as the special connotations of *ḥ-z-h* have disappeared (see above p. 27). This is strikingly evident in Jo 3:1 (MT; 2:28 in English versions), which says that in the last days, "young men will *see visions*" (*yir'û* from *r-'-h* with *ḥezyōnôt* from *ḥizzāyôn*, root *ḥ-z-h*). In this late text it is obvious that in the time of the author, *ḥizzāyôn* had already lost the connotation of a spoken word of God, so that the verb *rā'āh* was suitable for *ḥizzāyôn*. In the Book of Ezekiel however, terms from the roots *r-'-h* and *ḥ-z-h* are used in their original meaning.

The second objective of the present study investigated the use of the Thai term นิมิต (*nimit*) in the translation of the different Hebrew terms above by taking all occurrences of *nimit* in the THSV 2011 as a starting point. The following table summarizes the findings:

	Hebrew term	*occur-rence*	*THSV 2011*
ḥ	*ḥāzôn*	7	*nimit*
z	*maḥăzê*	1	*nimit*
h	*ḥāzâ (verb)*	6	*nimit*
	mar'ê	36	
r	*- without definite article*	30	*laksana*
'	*- with definite article*	6	*nimit*
h	*mar'â*	4	*nimit*

If one considers those research results, it is conspicuous that the Thai translation does not distinguish between the terms derived from *r-'-h* and *ḥ-z-h*; they do all get translated as *nimit*. In the Thai Bible there is no distinction whether the prophet sees visions or receives spoken messages from God. Although the term *ḥāzôn* in Ezekiel is used only outside the vision reports to express the fact that someone received has spoken messages from God, the Thai standard version still translates the term with *nimit* like the terms that are reserved for seen visions from God.[1] Further research will

[1] Although 2 Sam 7:17 does have yet another term that is derived from *ḥ-z-h* (*ḥizzāyôn*), it serves as a good illustration here. The reader might feel irritated when he reads that Nathan spoke to David in according

have to show if the Thai translation follows the English Bible; the fact however that terms like *ḥāzôn* and *maḥăzê* and other derivatives of *ḥ-z-h* are rendered as "vision" in Brown-Driver-Briggs's dictionary seems to point in this direction.[2]

On the other hand, the Thai translation is consistent when it comes to translate the term that makes up the vast majority of terms rendered as *nimit* in Thai: *mar'ê.* Whenever the Thai reader encounters the term *nimit* connected with a relative clause in the first person singular, the Hebrew term behind that translation is *mar'ê.* Furthermore, two of the visions are called according to the place where Ezekiel has received them: The "vision that I saw in the valley[3]" (8:4) and the "vision that I had seen by the Chebar canal" (43:3) refer to the opening vision of the book in Ez 1–3. "the vision that I had seen when he came to destroy the city" (Ez 43:3) is a reference to the vision report in Ez 8–11. Though it is still clear to the careful reader of the Thai Bible, that in Ezekiel there are at least two vision reports that stand out from the text. If one considers the particular language in the opening and closing sections of the vision reports with their motives (hand of Yahweh, spirit, change of location), it is quite clear for the reader of the Thai Bible where each of the four vision reports starts and ends.

In order to reach the third objective, the study has analyzed what happened when Ezekiel received a vision. In summary, research has shown that it is by Yahweh the prophet is given access to the heavenly world where he sees future events that will happen in Israel. In short; Except for Ez 8 all visions are related to the future of

---

with all this vision (*ḥizzāyôn*, Thai: *nimit*). In all the preceding verses, it is neither reported that Nathan saw a vision nor what Nathan saw. It is therefore better to understand *ḥizzāyôn* as a parallel term to *haddĕbārîm* and thus as a reference to spoken messages by God that Nathan has received.

[2] Brown / Driver / Briggs (eds.), *Hebrew and English Lexikon*, 302f.

[3] However, "valley" reminds the reader of Ez 37:1.

Israel. The future is already present in heaven, which presupposes that heavenly and earthly realm correspond to each other.

In regards to the last objective (develop concepts about how to communicate the findings to Thai Christians), the study has shown that many different ideas about *nimit* might occupy the heads of the Thai people. Whenever one teaches, preaches to them, or leads a discussion, it is necessary to give information about the historical background and the concepts behind the visions in the Book of Ezekiel. However, it is striking that the term *nimit*, generally speaking, catches some aspects of the concepts behind Ezekiel's visions: *nimit* refers to a thing to come in the future, be it positive or negative like the visions of Ezekiel (except for Ez 8). Besides that, according to the dictionary, *nimit* can be translated as "reason, cause"; which is close to the concept that the things Ezekiel sees in the heavenly realm, are somehow the cause or reason. Even though Yahweh surely is the initiator of the events to come, *nimit* as "reason, cause" catches the priority of the heavenly realm: events happen in heaven *first*, and then on earth afterwards (Mt 6:10 "on earth as it is in heaven"). Having summarized the findings of this study, the following paragraphs will make practical recommendations.

6.2 Recommendations

Given the fact that the word *nimit* in the Bible has such widely developed concepts in the background, it seems questionable whether the "organizational use" (p. 92) of *nimit* is useful and wise. To the author, it seems to be better to speak of วิสัยทัศน์ทัศน์ (*wisaithat*), which refers to the ability to see things that will happen in the future. This term is not a biblical term, and so avoids adding unnecessary confusion to the term *nimit*. Even better though, and easier to understand, is the Thai term เป้าหมาย (*paumay*) which simply means "aim" or "goal".

Secondly, anyone that wants to study the bible carefully in the Thai text should be aware that the term *nimit* is used uniformly in the Thai Bible. *Nimit* can refer to spoken words of God that a prophet has received - with no act of seeing involved. Or it denotes the visions that a prophet has seen. Depending on the context, the reader has to decide whether he deals with a *nimit* that someone has *heard*, or with a *nimit* that someone has *seen*. This approach is also sensitive to the efforts of the Bible translators and prevents against the accusation that one wants to criticize the Thai Bible or its translators for using a wrong or ambiguous term in translating the Bible.

6.3 Areas of Future Research

First of all, one has to keep in mind that the term *nimit* is possibly an important word in Buddhism. In Chiang Mai, the place where the author has been living for seven years, Buddhist temples frequently invite one to a "*fang luk nimit* ceremony": A large round object (usually twice as big in diameter as a football) that is covered with gold plates is buried in the ground. It seems as if these balls (in Thai *luk*) are meant as good omens that ensure the success, safety, and blessing of the building that is about to be built.

Further research has to clarify this and also investigate the use and the meaning of the term *nimit* in other Buddhist contexts.

Secondly, future research should build upon the observation that in later times, all of the special notions of *ḥ-z-h* and its derivatives have disappeared. When and why did this process start? Which texts, sections, or books of the Bible are still aware about the difference between *r-'-h* and *ḥ-z-h*? Further research could easily pick up other books of the Bible and study the use of *nimit* and its Hebrew counterparts in other texts in the Bible.

Finally, future researchers that lean on the more practical side of theology could possibly use the results of this study to develop teaching materials or a series of lessons. A possible outline to this might be (1) Ezekiel and his times (historical background of Ezekiel), (2) What happened when Ezekiel received a vision?, and (3) What is the meaning of the visions in Ezekiel?

Appendix 1: Tables

Table 1 *ḥāzôn* and *nimit* in Ezekiel
(see above p. 31ff.)

Ez	Hebrew	TSV 2011
7:13	*ḥāzôn*	นิมิต *nimit*
7:26	*ḥāzôn minnābî'*	นิมิตจากผู้เผยพระวจนะ *nimit chag phuphoeiphrawa-chana*
12:22	*ḥāzôn*	นิมิต *nimit*
12:23	*ḥăzôn*	นิมิต *nimit*
12:24	*ḥāzôn šāw'*	นิมิตปลอม *nimit plom*
12:27	*heḥāzôn ăšer hû' ḥōzê*	นิมิตที่เขาเห็น *nimit thi khau hen*
13:16	*ḥāzôn šālōm*	นิมิตแห่งสันติภาพ *nimit haeng santiphap*

Table 2 *mar'ê* and *nimit* in Ezekiel
(see above p. 33ff.)

Ez	Hebrew	TSV 2011
1:5	*mar'ê*[1]	ลักษณะ *laksana*

[1] + suffix 3. p. pl. *-hen*

1:13a	*mar'ê*[2] *kĕ*	ลักษณะ ... เหมือน ... *laksana ... muean ...*
1:13a	*kĕmar'ê*	ลักษณะเหมือน ... *laksana muean ...*
1:14	*kĕmar'ê*	เหมือนลักษณะ ... *muean laksana ...*
1:16a	*mar'ê ... kĕ*	ลักษณะ ... เหมือน ... *laksana ... muean ...*
1:16b	*mar'ê*[3] *... ka'ăšer*	ลักษณะ ... เหมือน ... *laksana ... muean ...*
1:26a	*kĕmar'ê*	ลักษณะเหมือน ... *laksana muean ...*
1:26b	*kĕmar'ê*	ลักษณะเหมือน ... *laksana muean*
1:27aα	*kĕmar'ê*	ลักษณะคล้าย ... *laksana khlay ...*
1:27aβ	*mar'ê*[4]	ลักษณะ *laksana*
1:27bα	*mar'ê*[5]	ลักษณะ *laksana*
1:27bβ	*kĕmar'ê*	ลักษณะคล้าย ... *laksana khlay...*
1:28aα	*kĕmar'ê*	เหมือนลักษณะ ... *muean laksana*
1:28aα	*mar'ê*	ลักษณะ *laksana*
1:28aβ	*mar'ê*	ลักษณะ *laksana*

---

[2] + suffix 3. p. pl. *-hen*

[3] + suffix 3. p. pl. *-hen*

[4] + prefixed *min-*

[5] + prefixed *ûmin-*

8:2aα	*kĕmar'ê*	* *not translated*
8:2aβ	*mar'ê*[6]	ลักษณะ *laksana*
8:2b	*kĕmar'ê*	ลักษณะ ... เหมือน ... *laksana muean*
8:4	*kammar'ê (+ article and relative clause)*	พระลักษณะเหมือน *phralaksana muean* (TSV 1971 นิมิต *nimit*)
10:1	*kĕmar'ê*	ลักษณะคล้าย ... *laksana khlay ...*
10:9	*mar'ê*[7] *... kĕ*	ลักษณะ ... เหมือน ... *laksana ... muean ...*
10:10	*mar'ê*[8]	* *not translated*
10:22	*mar'ê*[9]	ลักษณะ *laksana*
11:24a	*bammar'ê (+ article)*	นิมิต *nimit*
11:24b	*hammar'ê (+ article and relative clause)*	นิมิต *nimit*
23:15	*mar'ê*	เป็นเหมือน *pen muean*
23:16	*lĕmar'ê 'ênêhâ*	เมื่อเธอเห็นแล้ว *muea thoe hen laew*

6 + prefixed *min-*

7 + prefixed *û-*.

8 + prefixed *û-* and suffix 3. p. pl. *-hen.*

9 + suffix 3. p. pl. *-hen.*

40:3	*mar'ê*[10] *kĕmar'ê*	ลักษณะคล้าย ... *laksana khlay ...*
41:21	*hammar'ê kammar'ê*	ลักษณะเหมือน ... *laksana muean ...*
42:11	*kĕmar'ê*	ลักษณะเหมือน ... *laksana muean ...*
43:3aα[11]	*kĕmar'ê*[12]	ลักษณะ *laksana*
43:3aα	*hammar'ê (+ article and relative clause)*	นิมิต *nimit*
43:3aα	*kammar'ê (+ article and relative clause)*	นิมิต *nimit*
43:3aβ	*kammar'ê (+ article and relative clause)*	นิมิต *nimit*

Table 3 *mar'â* and *nimit* in Ezekiel
(see above p. 38f.)

Ez	Hebrew	TSV 2011
1:1	*wā'er'ê mar'ôt 'ĕlōhîm*	ข้าพเจ้าได้เห็นพระเจ้าในนิมิต *khapachao dai hen phrachao nai nimit*
8:3	*bĕmar'ôt 'ĕlōhîm*	ด้วยนิมิตของพระเจ้า *duay nimit khong phrachao*

[10] + suffix 3. p. sg. *-hû.*

[11] See Appendix 2, p. 106f.

[12] + prefixed *û-*.

40:2	*bĕmar'ôt 'ĕlōhîm*	โดยนิมิตของพระเจ้า *doy nimit khong phrachao*
43:3aβ[13]	*mar'ot*	และมีลักษณะ *lae mi laksana*

Table 4 The Verb *ḥāzâ* and *nimit* in Ezekiel
(see above p. 40ff.)

Ez	Hebrew	TSV 2011
13:6	*ḥāzû šāw'*	เขาทั้งหลายเห็นนิมิตปลอม *khathanglay hen minit plom*
13:8	*waḥăzîtem kāzāb*	เจ้าทั้งหลาย ... เห็นนิมิตเท็จ *chaothanglay ... hen nimit thed*
13:9	*haḥōzîm šāw'*	เห็นนิมิตปลอม *hen nimid plom*
13:23	*šāw' lō' teḥĕzênâ*	เจ้าจะไม่ได้เห็นนิมิตปลอม *chao ja mai hen nimit plom*
21:29 / **MT** 21:34	*baḥăzôt lāk šāw'*	เขาให้นิมิตปลอมแก่เจ้า *khau hai nimit plom gae chao*
22:28	*ḥōzîm šāw'*	การเห็นนิมิตปลอม *gan hen nimit plom*

[13] See Appendix 2, p. 106f.

Appendix 2: *mar'ê* and *mar'ah* in Ez 43:3

aα *ûkĕmar'ê hammar'ê 'ăšer rā'îtî*
aβ *kammar'ê 'ăšer-rā'îtî bĕbō'î*[1] *lĕšaḥēt*
bα *ûmar'ôt kammar'ê 'ăšer rā'îtî 'el-nĕhar-kĕbâr*
bβ *wâ'eppōl 'el-pânāyw* (MT)

aα และนิมิตที่ข้าพเจ้าเห็นนั้น มีลักษณะ
lae nimit thi khapchao hen nan mi laksana
aβ เหมือนนิมิตซึ่งข้าพเจ้าเห็นเมื่อพระองค์เสด็จมาทำลายเมืองนั้น
muean nimit sueng khapchao hen muea phraong sadet ma thamlai mueang nan
bα และมีลักษณะเหมือนนิมิตซึ่งข้าพเจ้าได้เห็นที่ริมแม่น้ำเคบาร์
lae mi laksana muean nimit sueng khapchao da hen thi rim mae nam khebar
bβ แล้วข้าพเจ้าก็ซบหน้าลงถึงดิน
laew khapchao go sob na long din (TSV 2011)

aα And the vision I saw was just
aβ like the vision that I had seen when he came to destroy the city,
bα and just like the vision that I had seen by the Chebar canal.
bβ And I fell on my face. (ESV)

Following LXX, Zimmerli[2] and Allen[3] have suggested to delete the first word in the text (*ûkĕmar'ê*). To the author, however, it seems best to keep it and see *mar'ê* in combination with the genitive object *hammar'ê 'ăšer rā'îtî*: "and the appearance *of* the vision that I saw". *mar'ê* (מַרְאֵה) is the construct state of *mar'ê* (מַרְאֶה) and

---

[1] *bĕbō'î* ("when I came to destroy") is probably an error for *bĕbō'ô* ("when he came to destroy), cf. Block, *The Book of Ezekiel: Chapters 25–48* (NICOT), 574.

[2] Zimmerli, *Ezekiel 2* (Hermeneia) 407.

[3] Allen, *Ezekiel 20–48* (WBC 29), 242.

clearly indicates a following genitive object. After that, both the Thai and English insert “was” or “has been” (มี mi). The *kĕ* in the first word of the sentence does not need to be translated, as it corresponds to the *kĕ* in *kammar’ê*. The construction *kĕ... kĕ* appears frequently in the Old Testament.[4]

In the second half of the sentence, *ûmar’ôt* is often understood as an addition in the Hebrew text and thus does not have to be translated.[5] If we want to keep *ûmar’ôt* however, it should be translated as “visions”. We thus get the following raw translations:

> “And the appearance of the vision that I saw [was] like the vision that I had seen when he came to destroy the city and the visions [were] like the vision that I had seen by the Chebar canal.”
>
> และลักษณะของนิมิตที่ข้าพเจ้าเห็นนั้น เหมือนนิมิตซึ่งข้าพเจ้าเห็นเมื่อพระองค์เสด็จมาทำลายเมืองนั้น และนิมิตเหมือนนิมิตซึ่งข้าพเจ้า ได้เห็นที่ริมแม่น้ำเคบาร์
>
> *lae laksana khong nimit thi khapchao hen nan muean nimit sueng khapchao hen muea phraong sadet ma thamlai mueang nan lae nimit muean nimit sueng khapchao dai hen thi rim maenam khebar*

ESV however has chosen to omit *ûkĕmar’ê* in the beginning of the verse and thus translates: “*And the vision that I saw was just like the vision that I had seen when he came to destroy the city*." In the second half, ESV has omitted *ûmar’ôt* as well: Out of five forms of *mar’ê* and *mar’ah*, only three are translated.

---

[4] Block, *The Book of Ezekiel: Chapters 25–48* (NICOT), 574 lists numerous examples, among them Ez 16:44.

[5] Allen, *Ezekiel 20–48* (WBC 29), 242; Block, *The Book of Ezekiel: Chapters 25–48* (NICOT), 574.

The TSV 2011 is going a different way than the ESV and sticks closer to the Hebrew. Firstly, it has slightly changed the word order:

> และนิมิตที่ข้าพเจ้าเห็นนั้นมีลักษณะเหมือนนิมิตซึ่งข้าพเจ้าเห็นเมื่อพระองค์เสด็จมาทำลายเมืองนั้น
>
> *lae nimit thi khapchao hen nan mi laksana muean nimit sueng khapchao hen muea phraong sadet ma thamlai mueang nan*

In the second half, it looks like as if the TSV 2011 has translated *ûmar'ôt* as และมีลักษณะ (*lae mi laksana*):

> และมีลักษณะเหมือนนิมิตซึ่งข้าพเจ้าได้เห็นที่ริมแม่น้ำเคบาร์
> *lae mi laksana muean nimit sueng khapchao dai hen thi rim maenam khebar.*

Bibliography

Allen, Leslie C. *Ezekiel 20–48*. Word Biblical Commentary 29. Dallas: Word Books, 1990.

______. *Ezekiel 1–19*. Word Biblical Commentary 28. Dallas: Word Books, 1994.

Bartelmus, Rüdiger. *Einführung in das Biblische Hebräisch. Mit einem Anhang Biblisches Aramäisch*. Zürich: Theologischer Verlag, ^{2}2009.

Behrens, Achim. *Prophetische Visionsschilderungen im Alten Testament: Sprachliche Eigenarten, Funktion und Geschichte einer Gattung*. Alter Orient und Altes Testament 292. Münster: Ugarit-Verlag, 2002.

BibleWorks 9 Software for Biblical Exegesis & Research. Norfolk: BibleWorks, 2011.

Blenkinsopp, Joseph. *Ezekiel*. Interpretation. Louisville: John Knox Press, 1990.

Block, Daniel I. *The Book of Ezekiel: Chapters 1–24*. New International Commentary on the Old Testament. Grand Rapids: Eerdmans, 1997.

______. *The Book of Ezekiel. Chapters 25–48*. New International Commentary on the Old Testament. Grand Rapids: Eerdmans, 1998.

Brown, Francis, Driver, S. R. and Briggs, Charles A., (eds.) *Hebrew and English Lexikon of the Old Testament with an Appendix Containing the Biblical Aramaic*. Oxford: Clarendon Press, 1974.

Brownlee, William H. *Ezekiel 1–19*. Word Biblical Commentary 28. Waco: Word Books, 1986.

Bruce, Frederick F. *The Book of Hebrews*. The New International Commentary on the New Testament. Grand Rapids and Cambridge: Eerdmans, 1990.

Busink, Th. A. *Der Tempel von Jerusalem von Salomon bis Herodes. Eine archäologisch-historische Studie unter Berücksichtigung des westsemitischen Tempelbaus. 1. Band: Der Tempel Salomos*. Leiden/Boston: Brill, 1970.

Busink, Th. A. *Der Tempel von Jerusalem von Salomon bis Herodes. Eine archäologisch-historische Studie unter Berücksichtigung des westsemitischen Tempelbaus. 2. Band: Von Ezechiel bis Middot*. Leiden/Boston: Brill, 1980.

Collins, Billie Jean and Society of Biblical Literature. *The SBL Handbook of Style*. 2nd ed. Atlanta: SBL Press, 2014.

Cooke, G. A. *A Critical and Exegetical Commentary on the Book of Ezekiel*. The International Critical Commentary. Edinburgh: T. & T. Clark, 1985.

Cook, Stephen L. *Ezekiel 38-48: A New Translation with Introduction and Commentary*. The Anchor Yale Bible Commentaries. New Haven: Yale University Press, 2018.

Cooper, Lamar E. *Ezekiel*. The New American Commentary 17. Nashville: B&H Books, 1994.

Drinkard Jr., Joel F. "Throne." In: *The New Interpreters® Dictionary of the Bible* 5, edited by Katharine Doob Sakenfeld et al., 589-590. Nashville: Abingdon Press, 2009.

Eichrodt, Walther. *Ezekiel. A Commentary.* The Old Testament Library. London: SCM Press, 1970.

Eising, Hermann. “נְאֻם ne’um.“ In *Theological Dictionary of the Old Testament* 9, edited by Johannes G. Botterweck, Helmer Ringgren and Heinz-Josef Fabry, 109-113. Grand Rapids: William B. Eerdmans, 1998.

Elliger, Karl, and Rudolph, Wilhelm, eds. *Biblia Hebraica Stuttgartensia.* Stuttgart: Deutsche Bibelgesellschaft, 1977.

Fabry, Heinz-Joseph. “כִּסֵּה kissē’.” In *Theological Dictionary of the Old Testament* 7, edited by Johannes G. Botterweck, Helmer Ringgren and Heinz-Josef Fabry, 232-259. Grand Rapids: William B. Eerdmans, 1995.

Förg, Florian. “Present or Future Eschatology in Psalm 96 in the Light of Deutero-Isaiah.” *Journal of Biblical Text Research* 36 (2015): 270-285.

______. “The Origins of Old Testament Apocalyptic Literature.” In *Asia Journal of Theology* 31/2 (Oct. 2017): 55-76.

Fuhs, Hans F. “רָאָה ra’ah.“ In *Theological Dictionary of the Old Testament* 13, edited by Johannes G. Botterweck, Helmer Ringgren and Heinz-Josef Fabry, 208-242. Grand Rapids: William B. Eerdmans, 2004.

Greenberg, Moshe. *Ezekiel 1–20. A New Translation with Introduction and Commentary.* Anchor Bible 22. Garden City: Doubleday, 1983.

______. *Ezekiel 21–37. A New Translation with Introduction and Commentary.* Anchor Bible 22A. New York: Doubleday, 1997.

Hagner, Donald A. *Encountering the Book of Hebrews: An Exposition*. Encountering Biblical Studies. Grand Rapids: Baker Academic, 2002.

Hals, Roland M. *Ezekiel*. Forms of Old Testament Literature 19. Grand Rapids: Eerdmans, 1989.

Heinze, Ruth-Inge. *Trance and Healing in Southeast Asia Today*. Bangkok: White Lotus, 1988.

Heiser, Michael. *The Unseen Realm. Recovering the Supernatural Worldview of the Bible*. Bellingham: Lexham Press, 2015.

Hengel, Martin. *Judentum und Hellenismus. Studien zu ihrer Begegnung unter besonderer Berücksichtigung Palästinas bis zur Mitte des 2. Jh. v. Chr.* Wissenschaftliche Untersuchungen zum Neuen Testament 10. Tübingen: J.C.B. Mohr, 1969.

Horn, Ernst. *Von Schlangen, Geistern und liebenswerten Menschen: Heiteres und Nachdenkliches aus Thailand, dem Land der Freien*. Phayao: eg-Verlag, 2017.

Hoskin, John and Dugast, Jean-Léo. *The Supernatural in Thai Life*. Bangkok: Tamarind Press, 1993.

The Holy Bible, Thai Contemporary Version & New International Version. Bangkok: International Bible Society, 2007.

______. *Thai-English, Thai Standard Version & English Standard Version*. Bangkok: Thailand Bible Society, 2012.

Janowski, Bernd. „Die Heilige Wohnung des Höchsten. Kosmologische Implikationen der Jerusalemer Tempeltheologie.“ In *Der Gott des Lebens. Beiträge zur Theologie des Alten*

Testaments 3, 29-71. Neukirchen-Vluyn: Neukirchener Verlag, 2003.

Jepsen, Alfred. "חָזָה chāzāh." In *Theological Dictionary of the Old Testament* 4, edited by Johannes G. Botterweck, Helmer Ringgren and Heinz-Josef Fabry, 280-290. Grand Rapids: William B. Eerdmans, 1980.

Kessler, Rainer. *Sozialgeschichte des alten Israel. Eine Einführung.* Darmstadt: Wissenschaftliche Buchgesellschaft, 2006.

Klein, Ralph W. "Exile." In *The New Interpreters® Dictionary of the Bible* 2, edited by Katharine Doob Sakenfeld et al., 367-370. Nashville: Abingdon Press, 2009.

Koch, Klaus. "Das Reich der Heiligen und des Menschensohnes." In *Die Reiche der Welt und der kommende Menschensohn. Studien zum Danielbuch. Gesammelte Aufsätze Band 2*, edited by Martin Rösel, 140-172. Neukichen-Vluyn: Neukirchener Verlag, 1995.

Koehler, Ludwig and Baumgartner, Walter. *The Hebrew and Aramaic Lexicon of the Old Testament* 2, edited by M.E.J. Richardson. Leiden / New York / Köln: E.J Brill, 1995.

Lasor, William S. "Ezekiel IX. Alternative Views and Additional Information." In *The International Standard Bible Encyclopedia* 2, edited by Geoffrey W. Brownlee et al., 261-263. Grand Rapids: Eerdmans, 1982.

Longman, Tremper III and Raymond B. Dillard. *An Introduction to the Old Testament.* Grand Rapids: Zondervan, 2006.

Müller, Hans-Peter. "מַשָּׂא maśśā'." In *Theological Dictionary of the Old Testament* 9, edited by Johannes G. Botterweck,

Helmer Ringgren and Heinz-Joseph Fabry, 20-24. Grand Rapids: William B. Eerdmans, 1998.

Nichitoto, Robert. Concordance of the Thai Standard Version (1971) of the Bible. Bangkok: Thailand Bible Society, 1993 [in Thai].

Ottoson, M. "הֵיכָל hêkhāl." In *Theological Dictionary of the Old Testament* 3, edited by Johannes G. Botterweck and Helmer Ringgren, 382-388. Grand Rapids: William B. Eerdmans, 1978.

Pohlmann, Karl-F. *Das Buch des Propheten Hesekiel (Ezechiel) Kapitel 1-19 übersetzt und erklärt*. Altes Testament Deutsch 22/1. Göttingen: Vandenhoeck & Ruprecht, 1996.

Pohlmann, Karl-F. *Das Buch des Propheten Hesekiel (Ezechiel) Kapitel 20-48 übersetzt und erklärt*. Altes Testament Deutsch 22/2. Göttingen: Vandenhoeck & Ruprecht, 2001.

Riess, Jana. "Don't Read This Part Of The Bible If You're Under 30 (Or A Woman)". Blog. *Sojourners*, 2012. https://sojo.net/articles/don-t-read-part-bible-if-you-re-under-30-or-woman (accessed Oct. 3rd, 2018).

Royal Institute (ed.) *Royal Institute Dictionary, BE 2554 (2011), Commemorating His Majesty the King's 7th Cycle Birthday Anniversary, December 5, 2011*. Bangkok, Siriwathana Inter Print, 2011 [in Thai].

Russell, David S. *Between the Testaments*. SCM Press: London, 1960.

Scharrer, Immanuel. *An Introduction to the 16 Prophetical Books*. Chiang Mai: Faculty of Theology, Payap University, 1997 [in Thai].

Seow, Choon L. *A Grammar for Biblical Hebrew*. Nashville: Abingdon Press, 1995.

Stalker, D. M. G. *Ezekiel. Introduction and Commentary*. London: SCM Press, 1971.

Thiengburanathum, Wit. *Thai-English Dictionary (Library Edition)*. Bangkok: Ruamsan 1977.

Tuell, Steven S. "Ezekiel 40–42 as Verbal Icon." *The Catholic Biblical Quarterly* 58 (1996): 649-664.

Vetter, D. "רהא r'h sehen." In *Theologisches Handwörterbuch zum Alten Testament* 2, edited by Ernst Jenni and Claus Westermann, 692-701. 6th ed. Gütersloh: Chr. Kaiser/Gütersloher Verlagshaus, 2004.

Wallace, R. S. "Man." In *The Illustrated Bible Dictionary* 2, edited by J. D. Douglas, 940-942. Sydney / Auckland: Hodder & Stoughton, 1980.

Wallace, Daniel B., *Greek Grammar Beyond the Basics. An Exegetical Syntax of the New Testament*. Grand Rapids: Zondervan, 1996.

Waltke, Bruce K. and O'Connor, M. *An Introduction to Biblical Hebrew Syntax*. Winona Lake: Eisenbrauns, 1990.

Wevers, John W. *Ezekiel*. New Century Bible. London: Oliphants 1969.

Wolff, Hans W. *Anthropology of the Old Testament*. Philadelphia: Fortress Press, 1974.

Zimmerli, Walther. *Ezekiel 1. A Commentary on the Book of the Prophet Ezekiel, Chapters 1 –24*. Hermeneia, trans. R. E. Clements. Philadelphia: Fortress Press, 1979.

Zimmerli, Walther. *Ezekiel 2. A Commentary on the Book of the Prophet Ezekiel, Chapters 25–48*. Hermeneia, translated by J. D. Martin. Philadelphia: Fortress Press, 1983.

Dortmunder Beiträge zu Theologie und Religionspädagogik
Prof. Dr. Michael Basse und Prof. Dr. Thomas Pola

Janieta Bartz
Jugendpastoral auf neuen Wegen
Der XXVIII. Weltjugendtag in Rio de Janeiro und sein Beitrag für die Kirche vor Ort
Diese Arbeit lässt Jugendliche aus aller Welt im Rahmen des XXVIII. Weltjugendtages zu Wort kommen und liefert Impulse für die jugendpastorale Praxis.
„Sie ist theoretisch bestens fundiert und empirisch innovativ angelegt; die erzielten Befunde – auf der Basis von 1.351 Datensätzen! – werden so ausgewertet, dass nachvollziehbar wird, wie die befragten Jugendlichen die Wirklichkeit des WJT wahrgenommen haben und welche Perspektiven sich daraus für die Jugendpastoral ergeben. Das Ergebnis löst ein, was der Titel verspricht: ‚Jugendpastoral auf neuen Wegen'."
Prof. i. R. Dr. Dr. h. c. Norbert Mette
Janieta Bartz (Technische Universität Dortmund) forscht seit 2012 zu Pastoraltheologie, Religionsdidaktik und Inklusion.
Bd. 14, 2017, 260 S., 34,90 €, br., ISBN 978-3-643-13760 9

Arnold Huijgen; Cees-Jan Smits; Eberhard Lempp (Hg.)
Schuld und Freiheit
Festgabe für Gerard Cornelis den Hertog
Gerard C. den Hertog hat es als niederländischer Theologe verstanden, das Werk des deutschen Theologen Hans und Theologinnen zugänglich zu machen. Freunde aus dem Iwand-Kreis, internationale Kollegen und Weggefährten haben sich zusammengefunden, um den Hertog mit dieser Festgabe zur Emeritierung zu grüssen.
Der Titel „Schuld und Freiheit" gibt einen Hinweis auf zwei Themen, die Den Hertog in seinem Bedenken der Iwandschen Theologie ebenso wie in aktueller Vergegenwärtigung wohl am meisten am Herzen liegen.
Bd. 13, 2017, 272 S., 34,90 €, br., ISBN 978-3-643-13155-3

Bert Roebben; Katharina Kammeyer (Eds.)
Inclusive Religious Education
International Perspectives
Bd. 12, 2014, 240 S., 29,90 €, br., ISBN 978-3-643-90355-6

Florian Förg
Die Jahwe-König-Psalmen und die Apokalyptik
Bd. 11, 2012, 160 S., 19,90 €, br., ISBN 978-3-643-90276-4

Ekkehard Graf
Durch Leiden geprägt
Die gegenwärtigen Leidenserfahrungen der indischen Nethanja-Kirche mit einem Blick auf die paulinischen Gemeinden
Bd. 10, 2012, 344 S., 29,90 €, br., ISBN 978-3-643-11595-9

Wai-Kwong Sun
Der Idealmensch des Konfuzius in paulinischer Betrachtung
Bd. 9, 2011, 296 S., 34,90 €, br., ISBN 978-3-643-11448-8

Michael Basse (Hg.)
Calvin und seine Wirkungsgeschichte
Bd. 8, 2010, 264 S., 24,90 €, br., ISBN 978-3-643-10853-1

Bert Roebben
Seeking Sense in the City
European Perspectives on Religious Education
Bd. 7, 2. Aufl. 2013, 312 S., 29,90 €, br., ISBN 978-3-643-10321-5

LIT Verlag Berlin – Münster – Wien – Zürich – London
Auslieferung Deutschland / Österreich / Schweiz: siehe Impressumsseite

Beiträge zum Verstehen der Bibel / Contributions to Understanding the Bible
Prof. Dr. Manfred Oeming (Heidelberg), Prof. Dr. Dr. h. c. mult. Gerd Theißen (Heidelberg) und Prof. Dr. Moisés Moyordomo (Basel)

Viktor Ber (ed.)
Nomos and Violence
Dimensions in Bible and Theology
The present volume is concerned with the problem of violence as reflected in the biblical texts, in their reception and interpretation. The expression 'nomos' in the title of the book is understood in a broader sense, with reference to the concept of nomos as a 'world of right and wrong' (Robert Cover). Therefore, the authors of the book are concerned not only with the legal texts of the Pentateuch, but also with other parts of the Old Testament / Tanak. Most of the contributors explore the theme of violence by interpreting specific narrative, legal, prophetic, and sapiential passages. Others attempt to offer a more general theological evaluation of violence in the Bible, also with constant reference to the biblical texts.
Bd. 35, 2019, 216 S., 34,90 €, br., ISBN 978-3-643-90997-8

Steven Paas (ed.)
Israelism and the Place of Christ
Christocentric Interpretation of Biblical Prophecy
Bd. 34, 2017, 272 S., 34,90 €, br., ISBN 978-3-643-90981-7

Petr Sláma
New Theologies of the Old Testament and History
The Function of History in Modern Biblical Scholarship
Bd. 33, 2017, 298 S., 39,90 €, br., ISBN 978-3-643-90841-4

Ulrich Kellermann
Elia als Toralehrer und Versöhner
Mal 3,22-24 und das Motiv der Zuwendung der Herzen von Vätern und Söhnen durch Elia im frühen Judentum
Bd. 32, 2017, 192 S., 34,90 €, br., ISBN 978-3-643-13571-1

Monika Szarek
Ehe und Askese
Familienethos bei Paulus und Musonius
Bd. 31, 2016, 272 S., 34,90 €, br., ISBN 978-3-643-13422-6

Gerd Theißen
Veränderungspräsenz und Tabubruch
Die Ritualdynamik urchristlicher Sakramente
Bd. 30, 2017, 454 S., 59,90 €, br., ISBN 978-3-643-13454-7

Gerd Theißen; Lung Pun Common Chan; István Czachesz
Kontraintuitivität und Paradoxie
Zur kognitiven Analyse urchristlichen Glaubens
Bd. 29, 2017, 386 S., 34,90 €, br., ISBN 978-3-643-13324-3

Manfred Oeming; Petr Sláma (Eds.)
A King like All the Nations?
Kingdoms of Israel and Judah in the Bible and History
Bd. 28, 2015, 348 S., 39,90 €, br., ISBN 978-3-643-90674-8

Ruth Huppert
Israel steht auf
Eine Studie zu Bedeutung und Funktion von Ez 37,1-14 im Buch Ezechiel
Bd. 27, 2016, 354 S., 34,90 €, br., ISBN 978-3-643-12746-4

LIT Verlag Berlin – Münster – Wien – Zürich – London
Auslieferung Deutschland / Österreich / Schweiz: siehe Impressumsseite

Altes Testament und Moderne

begründet von Hans-Peter Müller (†), Michael Welker und Erich Zenger (†)
herausgegeben in Verbindung mit Andreas Schüle und Bernd Janowski
ab Band 24 Prof. Dr. Michaela Bauks (Koblenz), Prof. Dr. Ulrich Berges (Bonn),
Prof. Dr. Daniel Krochmalnik (Potsdam), Prof. Dr. Manfred Oeming (Heidelberg)

Alexander Massmann; Christopher B. Hays (eds.)
Deathless Hopes
Reinventions of Afterlife and Eschatological Beliefs
Questions of eternal life and a revolution of the human condition have been a continuing theme in many religions, notably in the Abrahamic faiths. In one way or another, "deathless hopes" continue to play a prominent role in today's public discourses. To understand the current significance of the issue, a thorough grasp of historical dynamics is required. This volume gives a representative overview of prominent traditions in the Hebrew Bible, Jewish Studies, contemporary ethics, theology, and anthropology, but also evaluates common questions afresh, suggesting new perspectives.
Bd. 31, 2018, 202 S., 39,90 €, br., ISBN 978-3-643-91033-2

Lilli Ohliger
Das Narrativ der Schöpfung
Zur Rezeption alttestamentlicher Schöpfungsmythen in ausgewählter neuerer Literatur
Bd. 30, 2018, 264 S., 39,90 €, br., ISBN 978-3-643-13902-3

Misook Lim
Königskritik und Königsideologie in Ps 44-46
Eine exegetische Untersuchung zum theologischen Sinn in den kompositorischen „Unterbrechungen" der Psalmen-Trias, gelesen in *lectio continua*, gedeutet nach dem Prinzip der *concatenatio*
Bd. 29, 2017, 296 S., 39,90 €, br., ISBN 978-3-643-13578-0

Aris Margianto
Antike Seelsorge heute?
Studien zum Umgang mit Verlust, Krankheit und Tod im Buch Hiob, in der modernen Seelsorge und bei HIV-Patienten in Indonesien
Bd. 28, 2016, 272 S., 34,90 €, br., ISBN 978-3-643-13028-0

Eva Jenny Korneck
Das Buch Hiob als pädagogisches Konzept
Die Rede von Gottes Allmacht in religiösen Bildungsprozessen
Bd. 27, 2014, 368 S., 39,90 €, br., ISBN 978-3-643-12570-5

Robert Abelava
Le motif de la fragilité de l'homme dans le Psaume 90
Une analyse sémantique et contextuelle
Bd. 26, 2013, 328 S., 29,90 €, br., ISBN 978-3-643-90347-1

Daniel Krochmalnik; Hans-Joachim Werner (Hg.)
50 Jahre Martin Buber Bibel
Internationales Symposium der Hochschule für Jüdische Studien Heidelberg und der Martin Buber-Gesellschaft
Bd. 25, 2014, 392 S., 29,90 €, br., ISBN 978-3-643-12150-9

Michaela Bauks; Ulrich Berges; Daniel Krochmalnik; Manfred Oeming
Neue Wege der Schriftauslegung
Bd. 24, 2019, 234 S., 29,90 €, br., ISBN 978-3-643-13089-1

LIT Verlag Berlin – Münster – Wien – Zürich – London
Auslieferung Deutschland / Österreich / Schweiz: siehe Impressumsseite

Bibel und Ethik

Prof. Dr. Sven van Meegen (DHBW Heidenheim), Prof. Dr. Eberhard Schockenhoff (Universität Freiburg), Prof. Dr. Josef Wehrle (Universität München) und

Josef Wehrle
Der Dekalog
Text, Theologie und Ethik
Der Dekalog, das „Zehnwort", gehört zu den bekanntesten Texten des Alten Testaments. Im Verlauf der Jahrhunderte entstanden unzählige Übersetzungen. Sie weichen oft stark vom hebräischen Originaltext ab. Die vorliegende Interpretation nimmt die Originaltexte als Grundlage. Sie lassen den Dekalog und seine wichtigen Aussagen in einem ganz neuen Licht erscheinen. Die theologische und ethische Relevanz wird transparenter. Die bleibend gültigen Aussagen gewinnen an Profil und Plausibilität. Jeder, der sich mit diesem großartigen Zeugnis Israels und seiner Bedeutung für unsere heutige Zeit befassen möchte, erhält durch die Lektüre dieses Buches fundierte Informationen und Anregungen für den wissenschaftlichen Diskurs, aber auch für die Schule, Erwachsenenbildung und für die Gemeindepastoral.
Bd. 7, 2015, 216 S., 29,90 €, br., ISBN 978-3-643-12855-3

Jorgiano dos Santos da Silva
Füllet die Erde und macht sie euch untertan! (Gen 1,28)
Strukturen einer alttestamentlich begründeten Schöpfungstheologie und deren Konsequenzen für eine biblisch orientierte Umweltethik
Das Thema Ökologie, Umweltethik und Schöpfungsverantwortung gewinnt seit der Umweltenzyklika *Laudato si'* auch im theologischen Bereich zunehmend an Relevanz. Eine theologische Umweltethik ist dann nur möglich, wenn es ihr gelingt, aus sozialethischer Perspektive die biblische Offenbarung zur Schöpfung mit exegetischer Fachkompetenz zu erschließen. Diese Aufgabe zu erfüllen, gilt als Anliegen dieses Buches. Zentrale Schöpfungsaussagen in alttestamentlichen Texten werden herausgearbeitet, gängige Vorurteile oberflächlicher Rezeptionen korrigiert und Perspektiven für die Umweltethik erschlossen.
Bd. 6, 2018, 320 S., 39,90 €, br., ISBN 978-3-643-14171-2

Sven van Meegen; Josef Wehrle (Hg.)
Macht und Ohnmacht in der Bibel
Prof. P. Dr. Otto Wahl SDB zu Ehren
Bd. 5, 2012, 192 S., 19,90 €, br., ISBN 978-3-643-11691-8

Josef Wehrle
Der leidende Mensch und der mitleidende Gott
Ein Beitrag zur Anthropologie und Theologie des Alten Testaments
Bd. 4, 2012, 232 S., 24,90 €, br., ISBN 978-3-643-11520-1

Sven van Meegen
Alttestamentliche Ethik als Grundlage einer heutigen Lebensethik
Ein Beitrag zum interreligiösen Dialog
Bd. 3, 2005, 440 S., 34,90 €, br., ISBN 3-8258-8316-7

Sven van Meegen; Markus Graulich (Hg.)
Menschen – Rechte
Theologische Perspektiven zum 60. Jahrestag der Proklamation der Allgemeinen Erklärung der Menschenrechte
Bd. 2, 2008, 168 S., 17,90 €, br., ISBN 978-3-8258-1494-6

Josef Wehrle; Sven van Meegen (Hg.)
Gottes Wort – unser Leben
Biblische Texte als Grundlage einer lebensbejahenden Ethik
Bd. 1, 2007, 240 S., 24,90 €, br., ISBN 978-3-8258-9350-7

LIT Verlag Berlin – Münster – Wien – Zürich – London
Auslieferung Deutschland / Österreich / Schweiz: siehe Impressumsseite